D1300018

Imprint

Holger Nils Pohl
Dellbrücker Hauptstraße 74
51069 Köln
Germany

100 People Drawings

Print: ISBN 978-3-9821200-4-1
Ebook: ISBN 978-3-9821200-6-5

100 PEOPLE DRAWINGS

I believe in the power of drawing. You can use it for a means of communication, for building your career, for therapy or even just for fun and pleasure.
After creating the two *100 Daily Drawings* books with all sorts of things you could draw could draw, Benjamin and I thought that it was time to dedicate a drawing book solely on the most complex thing that exists – people. Humans are complex in two ways: to understand, and often to draw.
We have tried to make it as easy as possible for you to follow along, with things progressively getting harder as you draw along. We've also taken the liberty to include all sorts of scenes from life in this book.
While you follow the drawings in this book with your pen in hand, appreciate your ability to draw. Don't judge yourself. Acknowledge and be thankful that you can grow personally with every single stroke you put on paper.

Yours,

DAY 1

Having a heart

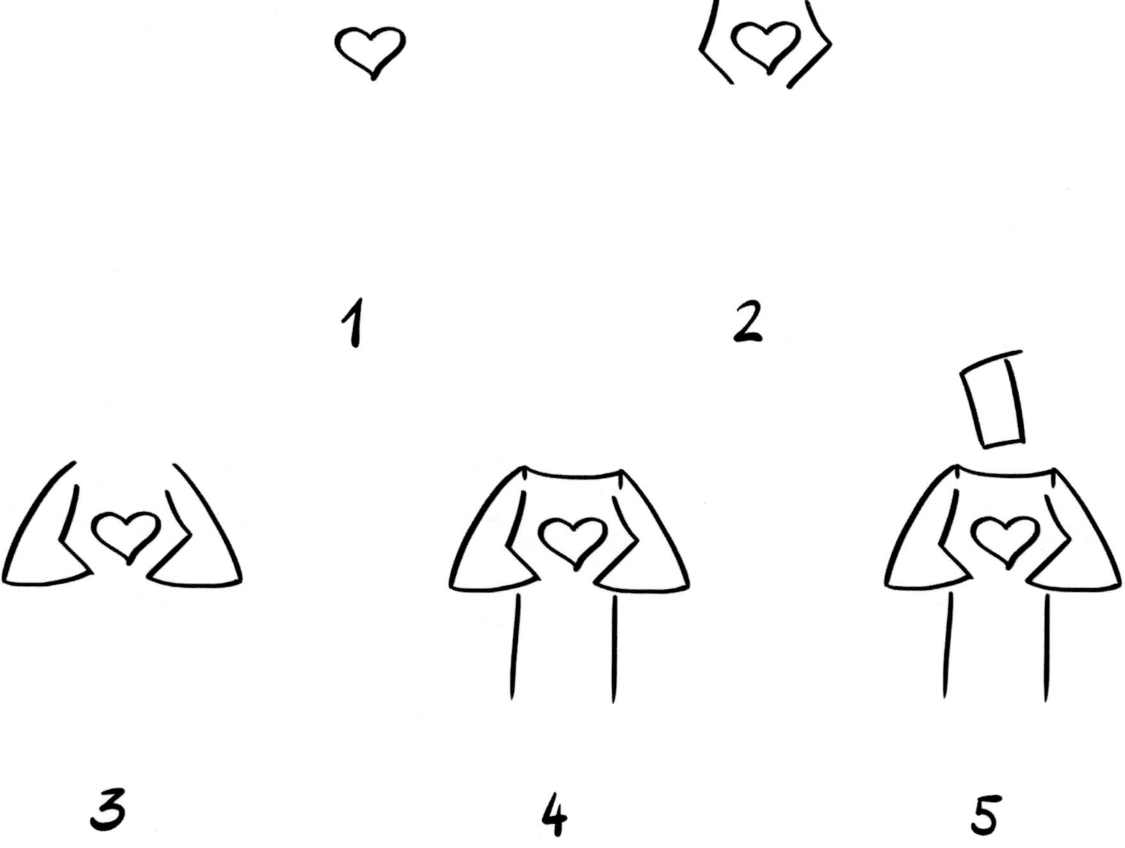

1
2
3
4
5

DAY 2

Crossing arms

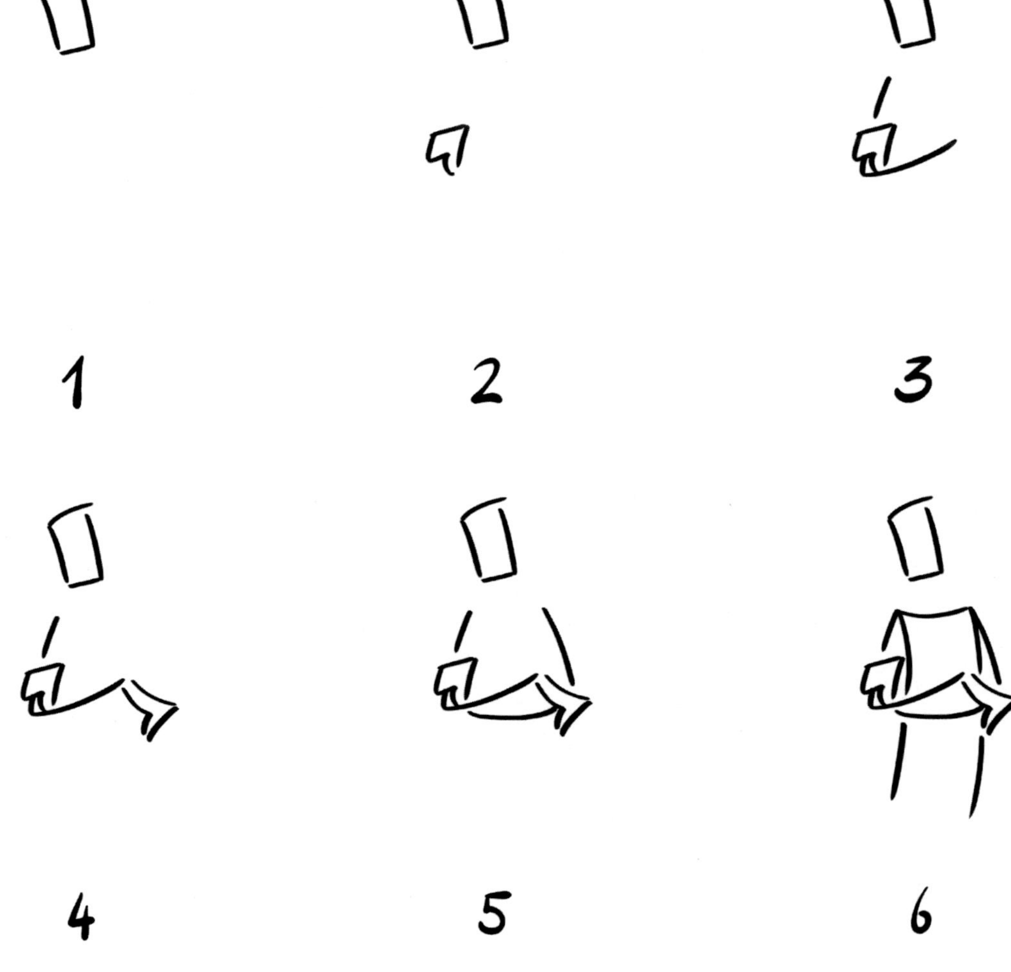
1
2
3
4
5
6

DAY 3

Signalling that someone is talking nonsense!

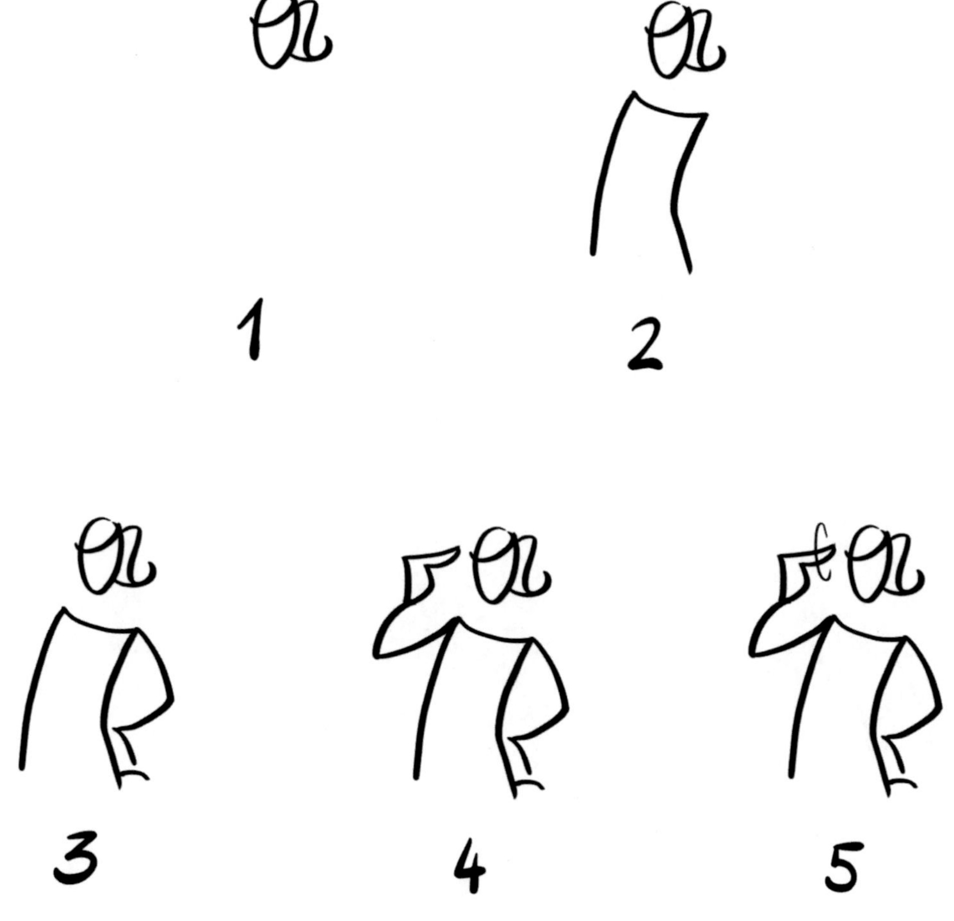

1
2
3
4
5

DAY 4

Blowing

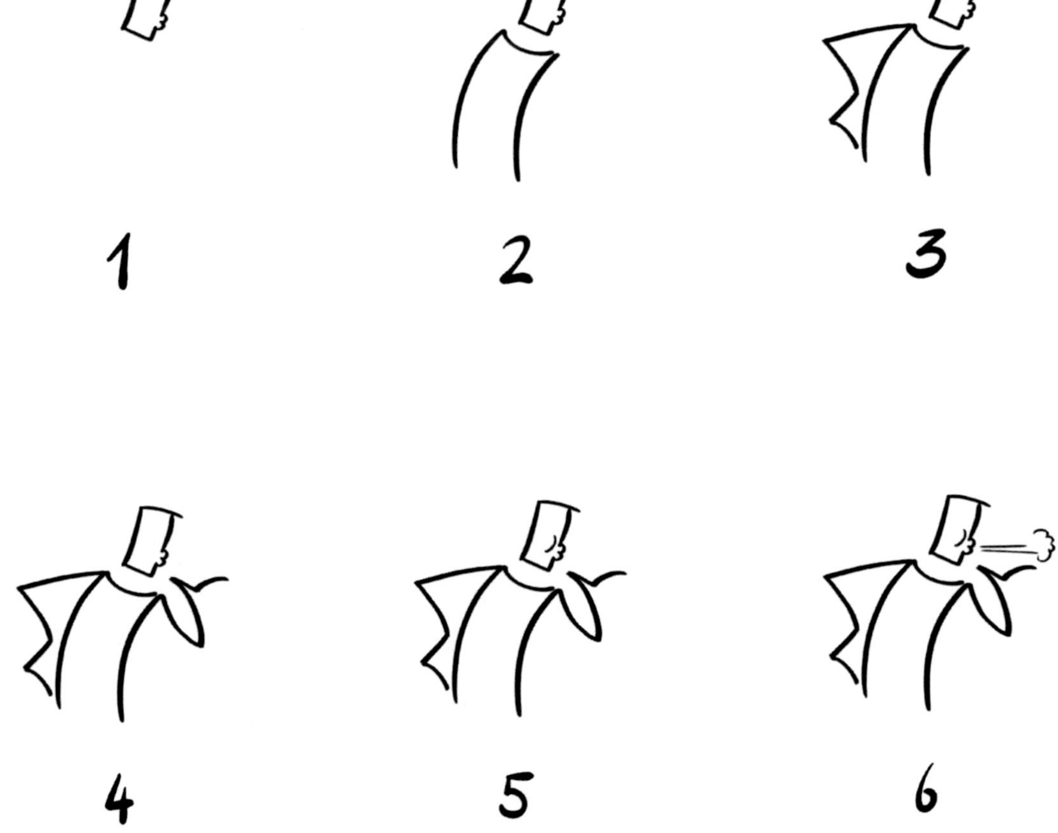
1
2
3
4
5
6

DAY 5

Stop!

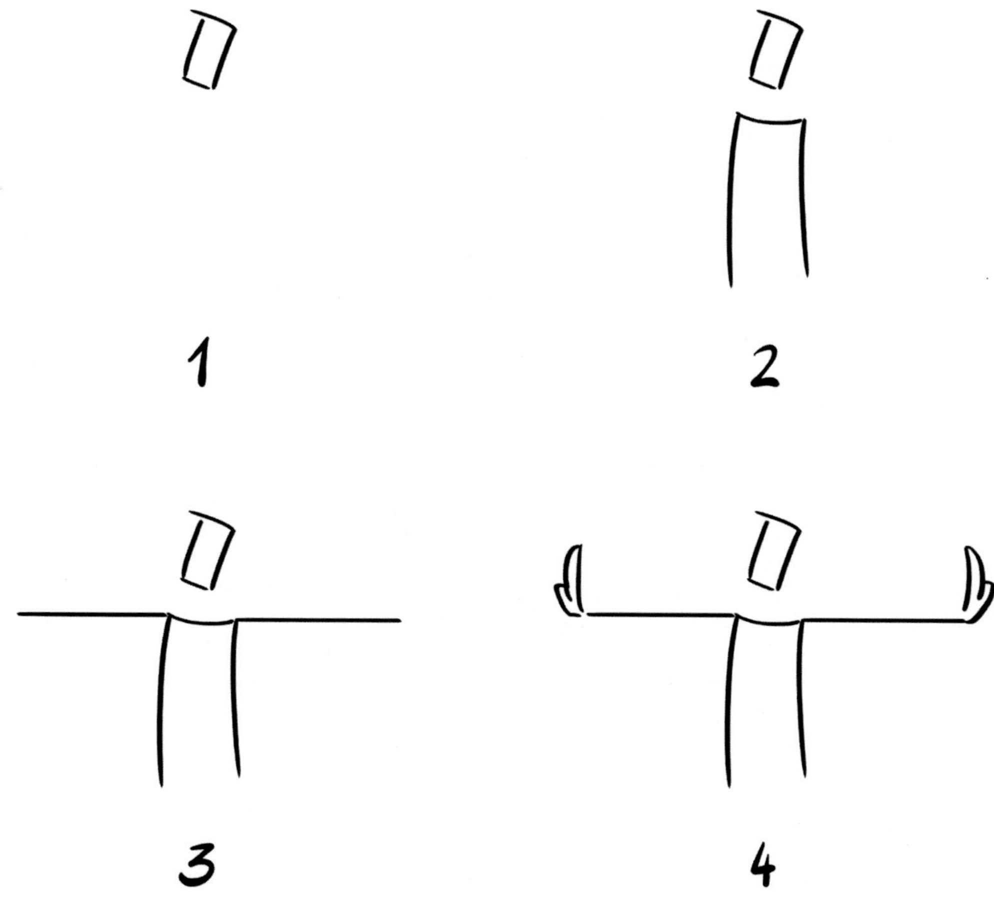

1
2
3
4

DAY 6

Waving goodbye

1
2
3
4
5
6

DAY 7

Snacking

1

2

3

4

5

6

DAY 8

Eating

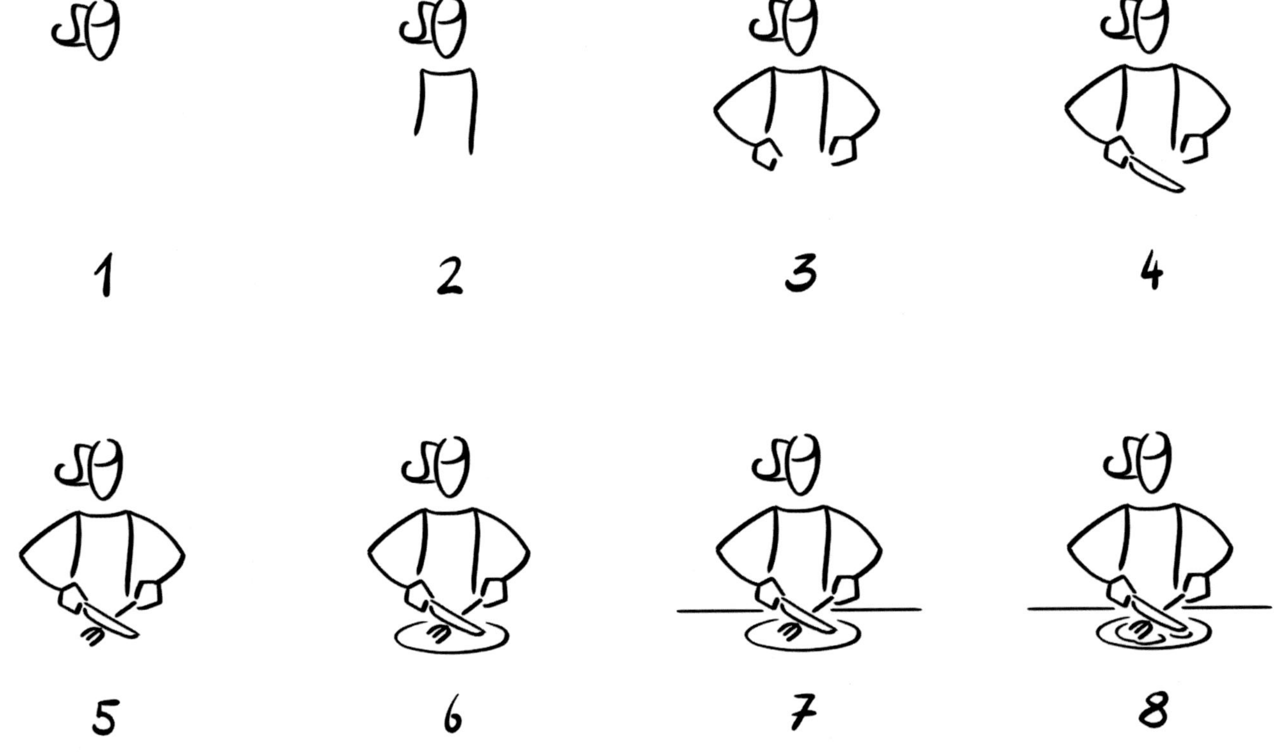

1
2
3
4
5
6
7
8

DAY 9

Reading a book

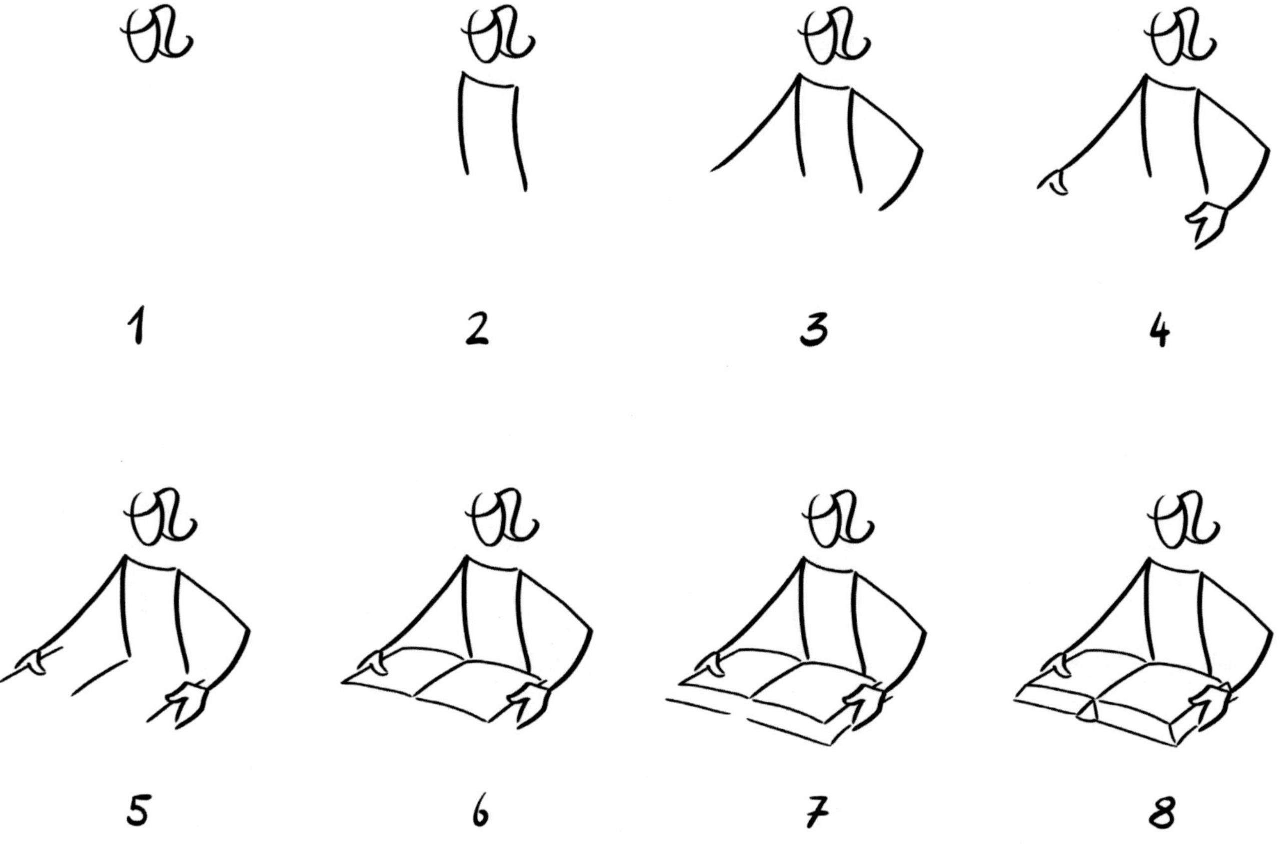

1
2
3
4
5
6
7
8

Texting

1

2

3

4

5

6

7

8

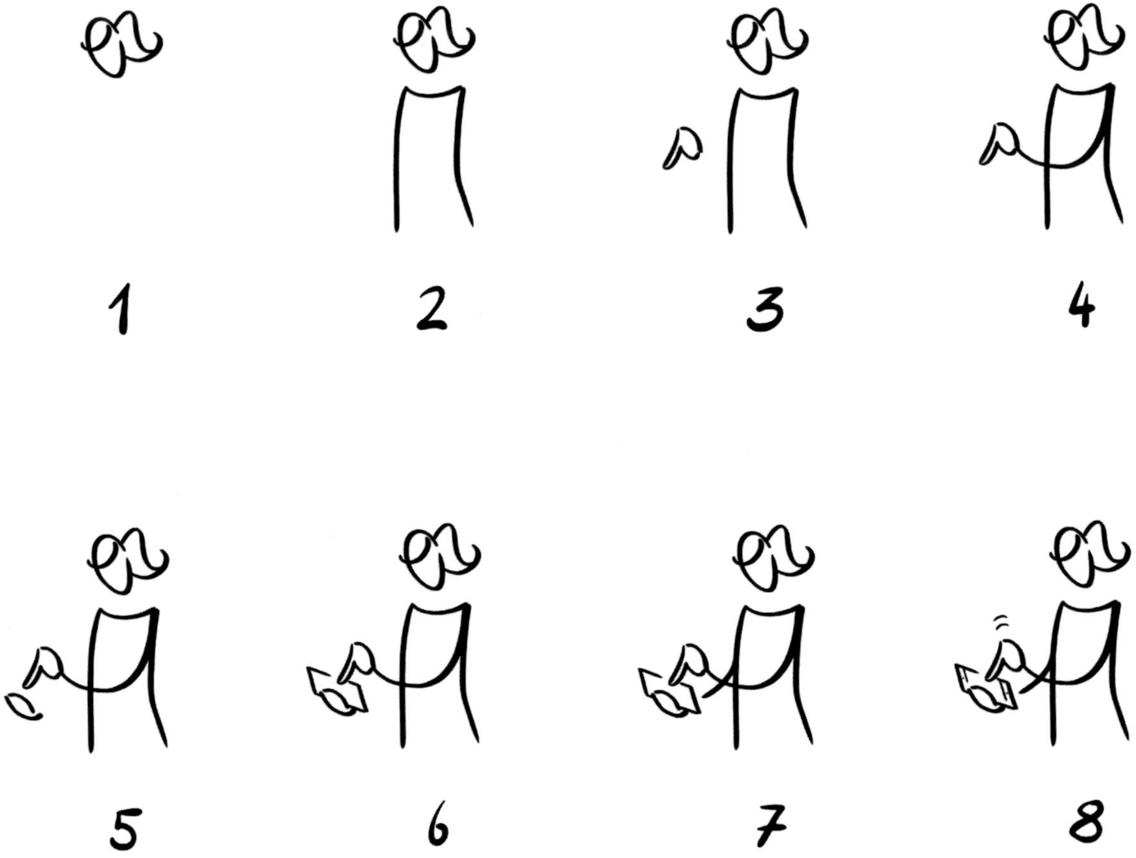

DAY 11

Falconry

1

2

3

4

5

6

7

8

9

DAY 12

Playing tambourine

1
2
3
4
5
6
7
8

DAY 13

Playing accordion

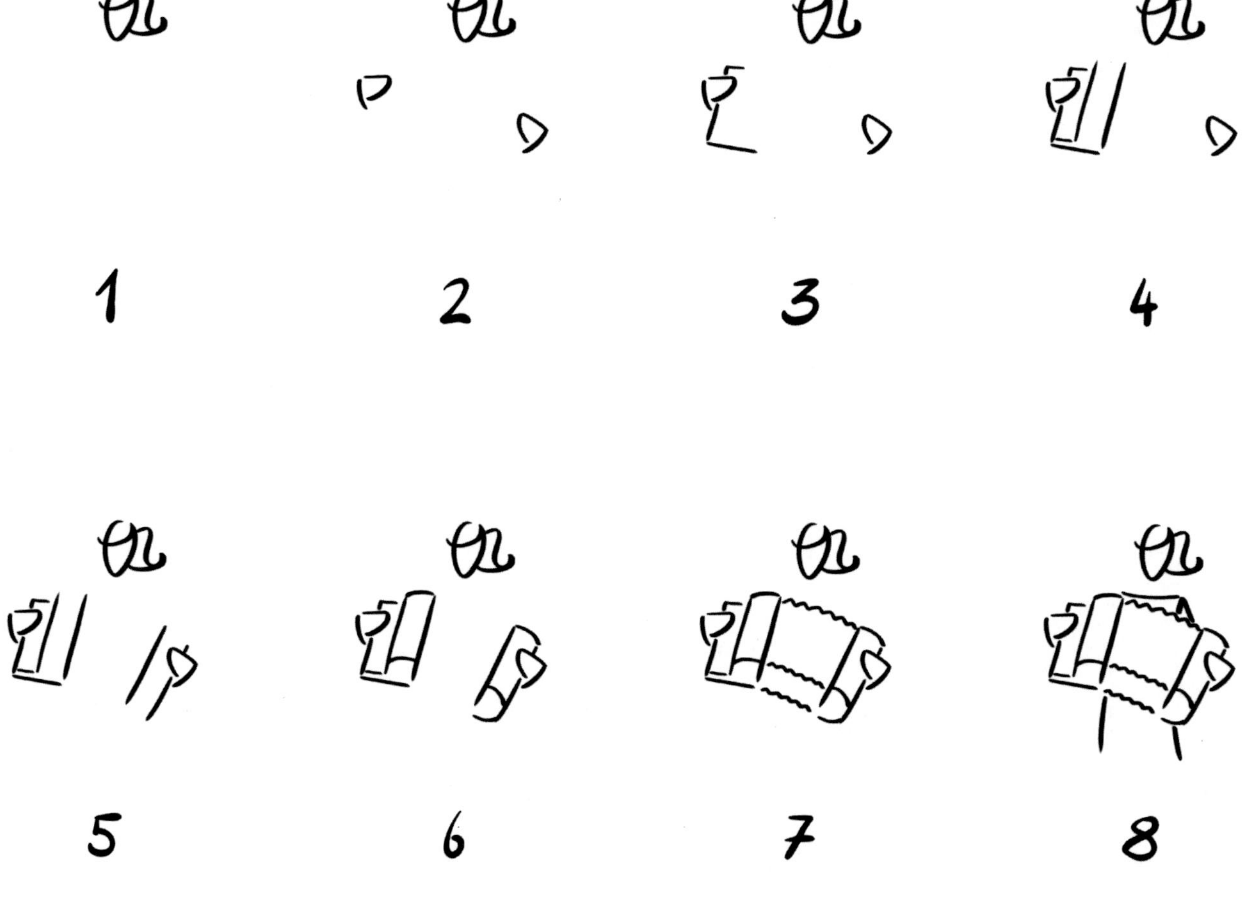
1
2
3
4
5
6
7
8

DAY 14

Giving the peace sign

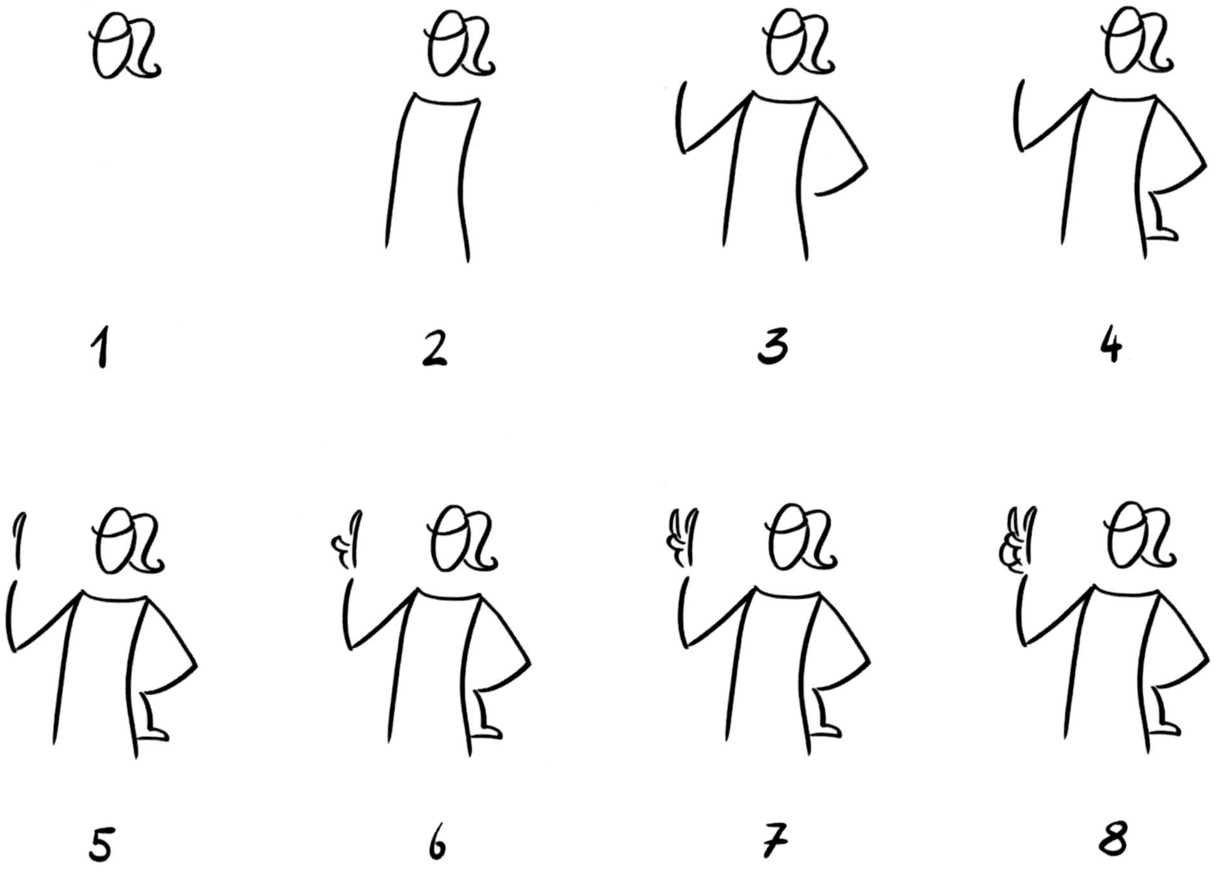

1

2

3

4

5

6

7

8

DAY 15

Using a magnifying glass

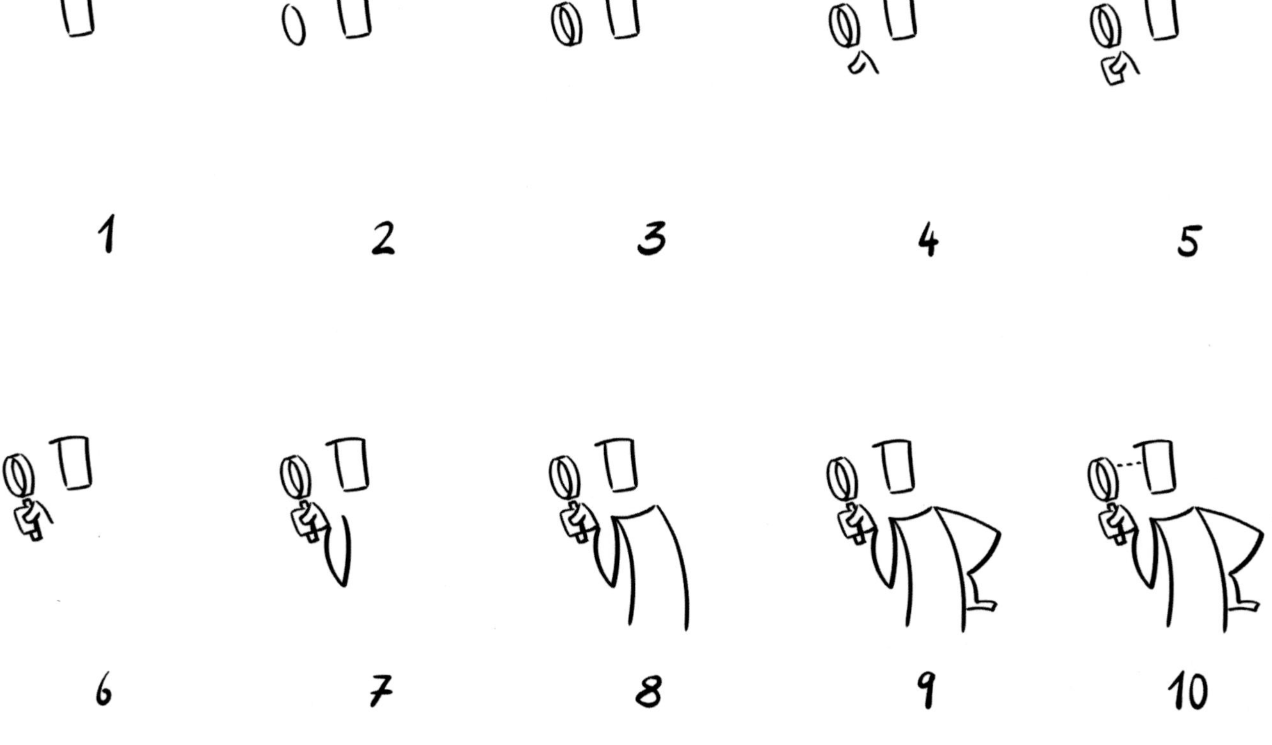
1
2
3
4
5
6
7
8
9
10

DAY 16

Reading the morning paper

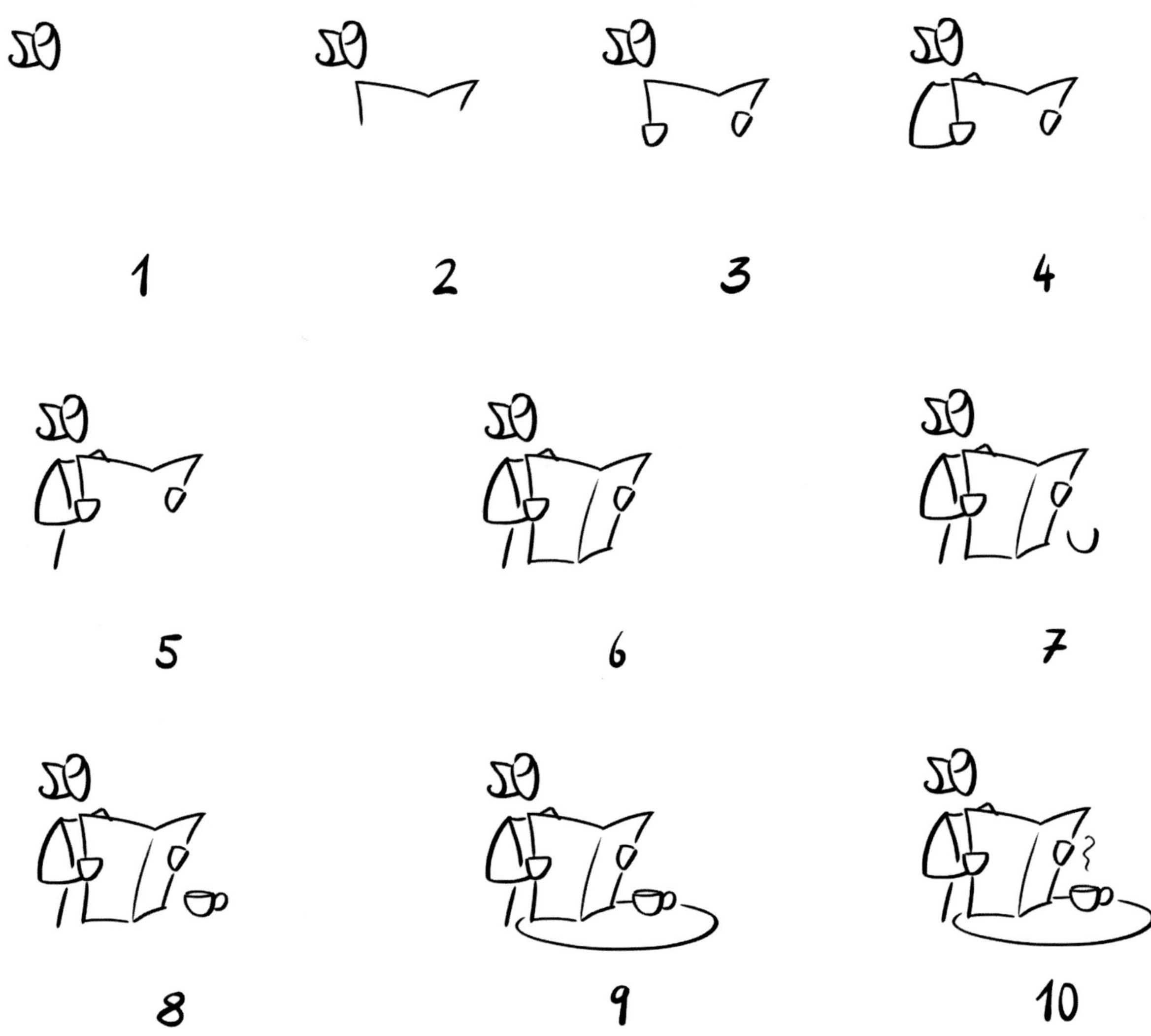

1
2
3
4
5
6
7
8
9
10

DAY 17

Mother carrying child

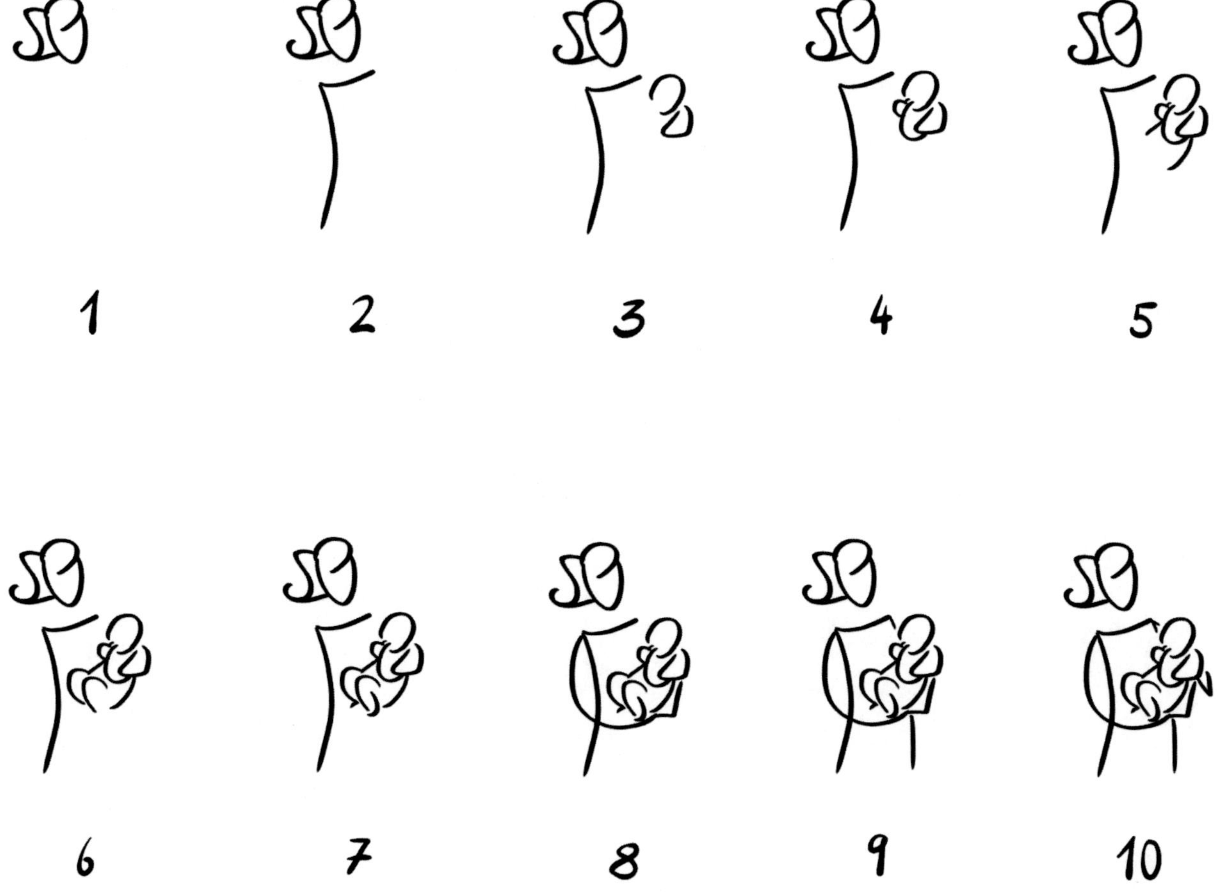
1
2
3
4
5
6
7
8
9
10

DAY 18

Cooking

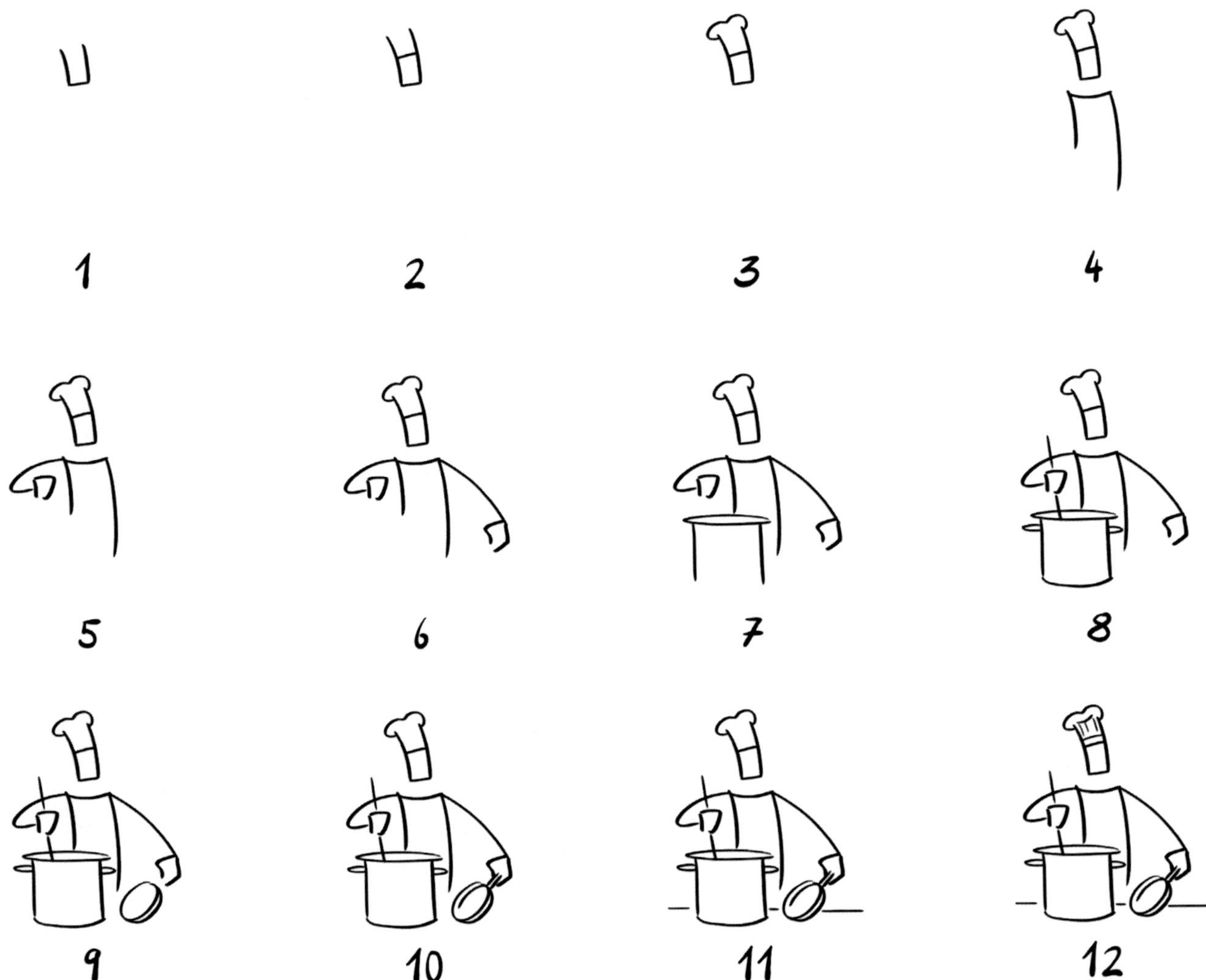

1
2
3
4
5
6
7
8
9
10
11
12

DAY 19

Shopping

1

2

3

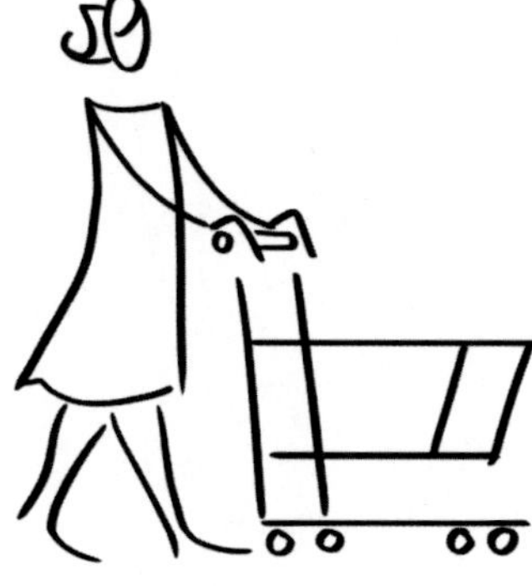

4

5

6

Shielding

1

2

3

4

5

6

7

8

DAY 21

Standing with a sword

1 2 3 4

5 6 7 8

DAY 22

Watching

1

2

3

4

5

6

7

8

DAY 23

Walking blindfolded

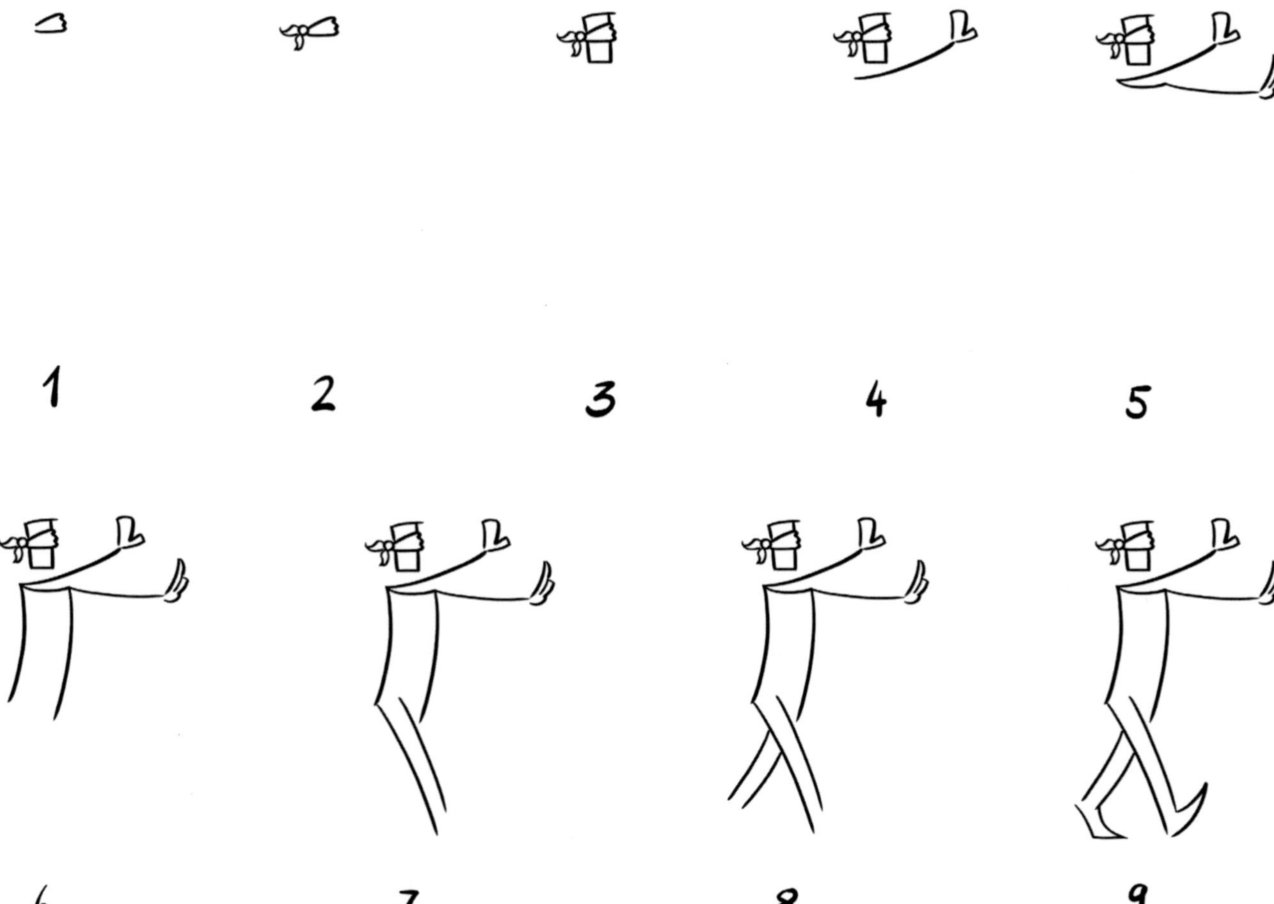
1
2
3
4
5
6
7
8
9

DAY 24

Practicing yoga

1

2

3

4

5

6

7

8

DAY 25

Flexing muscle

1

2

3

4

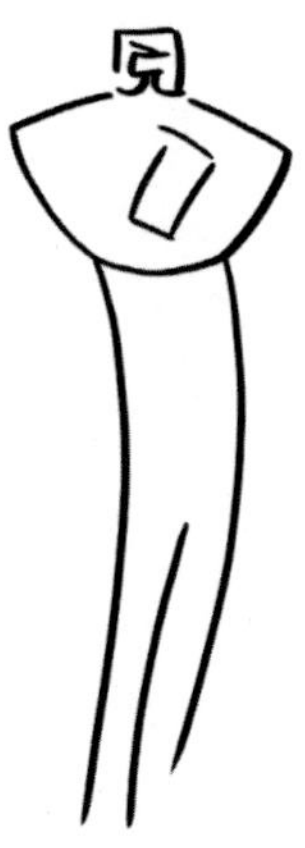

5

6

7

8

DAY 26

Doing a handstand

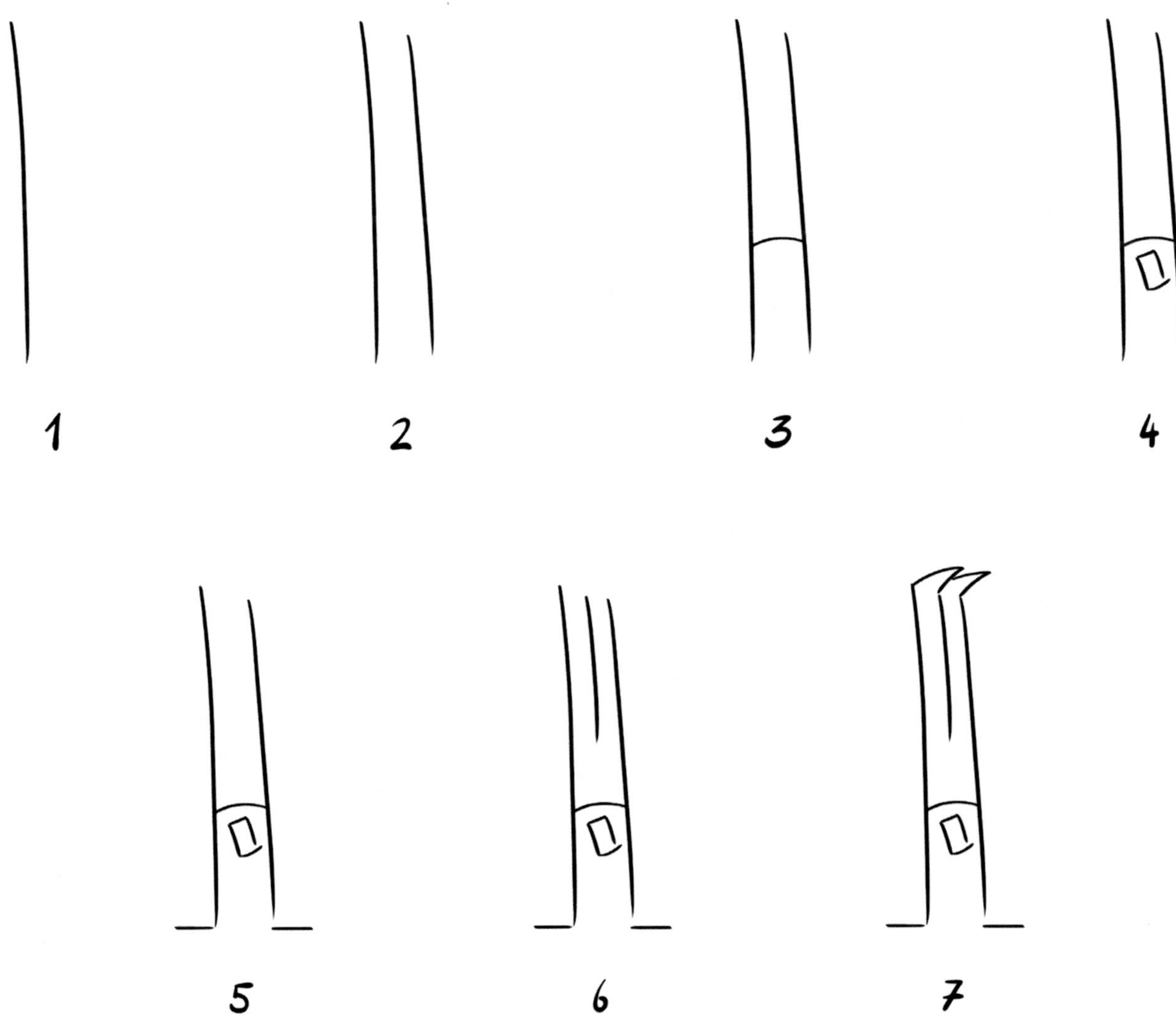
1
2
3
4
5
6
7

DAY 27

Juggling

1

2

3

4

5

6

7

8

DAY 28

Leaning

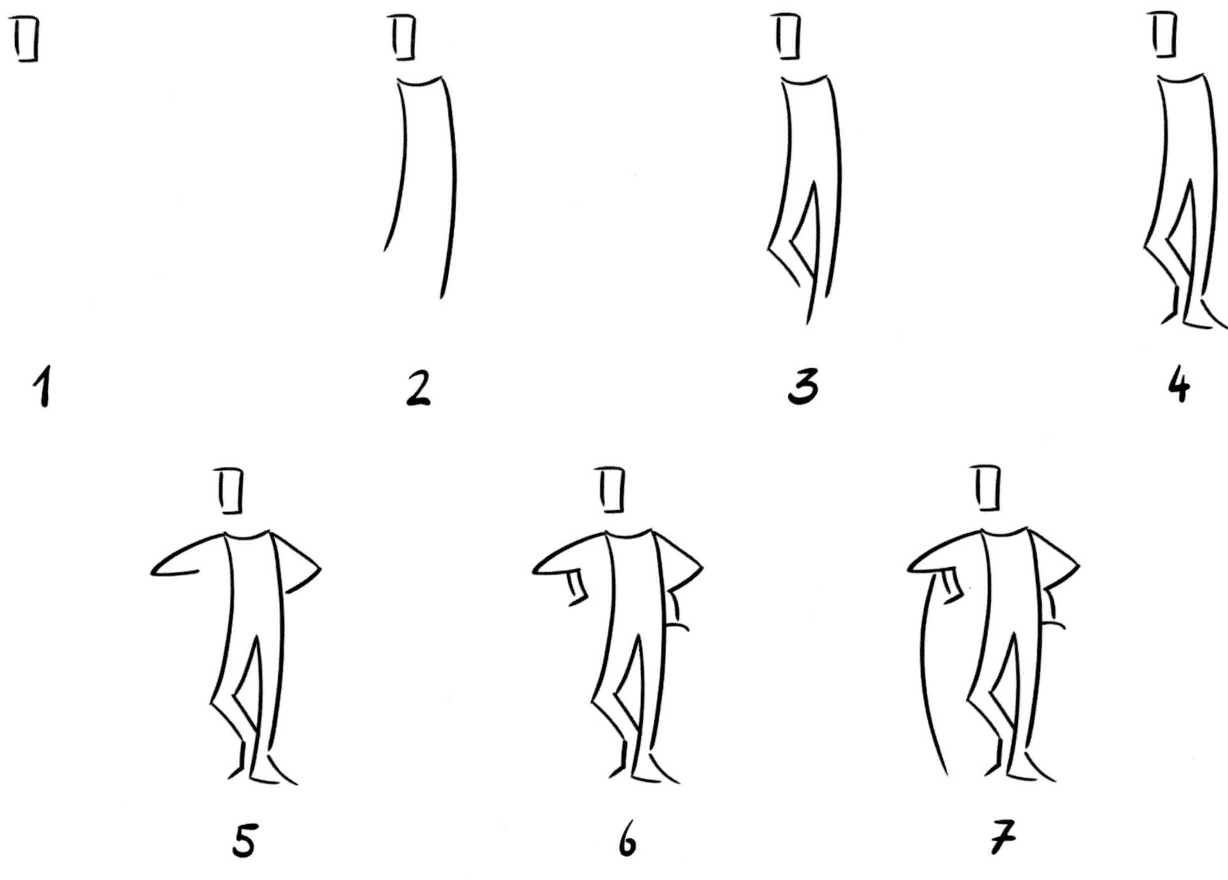

1
2
3
4
5
6
7

DAY 29

Watering plants

1

2

3

4

5

6

7

8

DAY 30

Being clueless

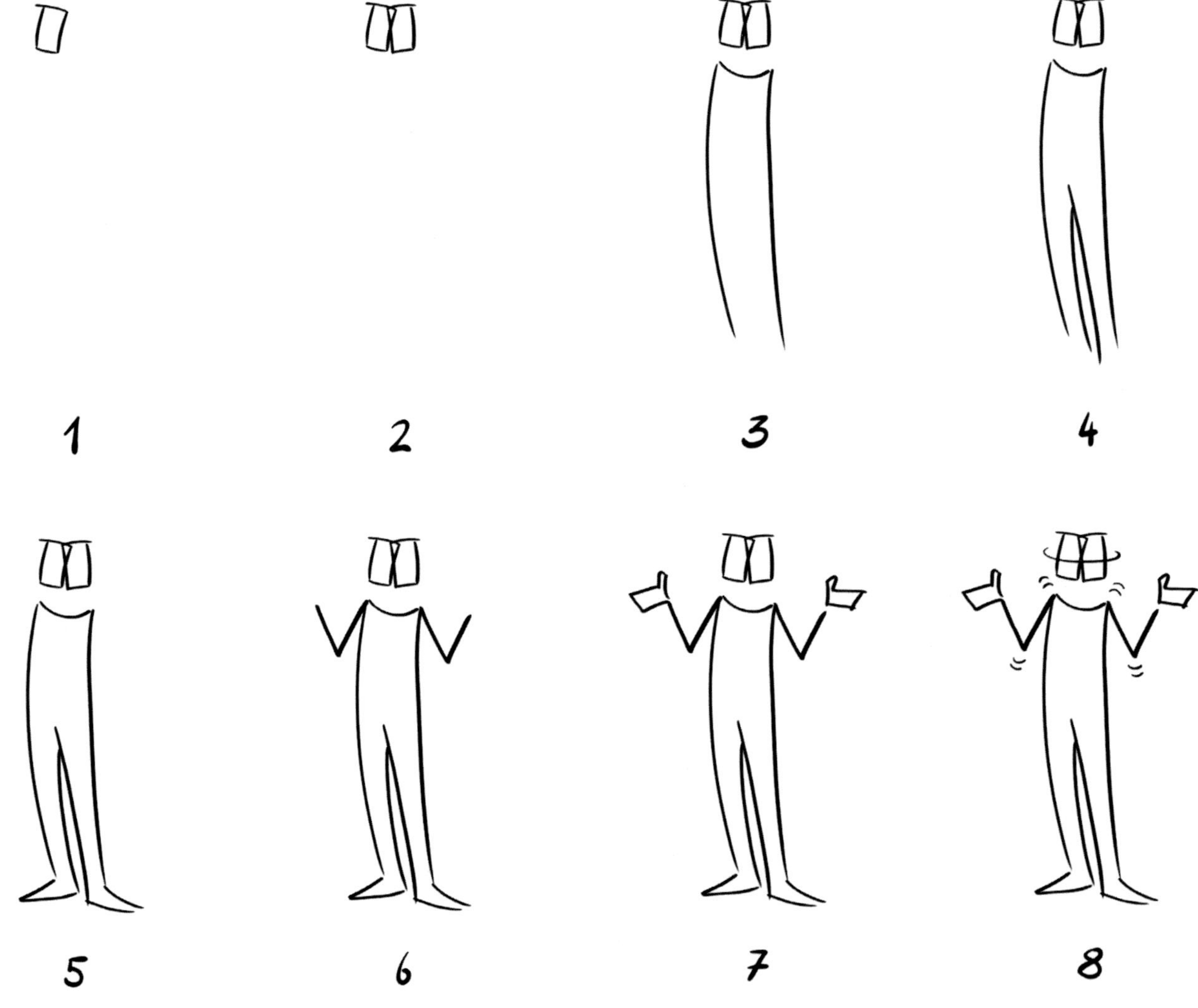

1
2
3
4
5
6
7
8

Sitting on the floor

1
2
3
4
5
6

DAY 32

Relaxing

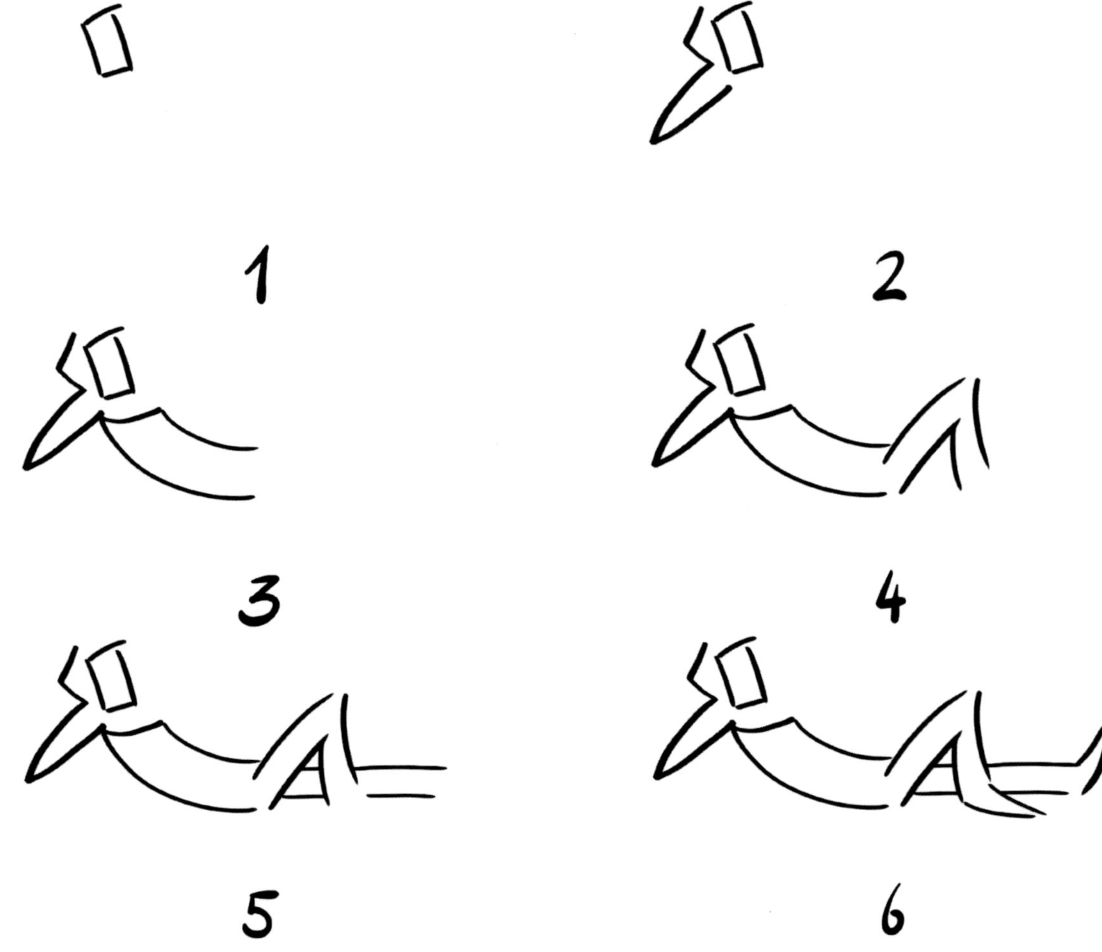

1
2
3
4
5
6

DAY 33

Down on one knee

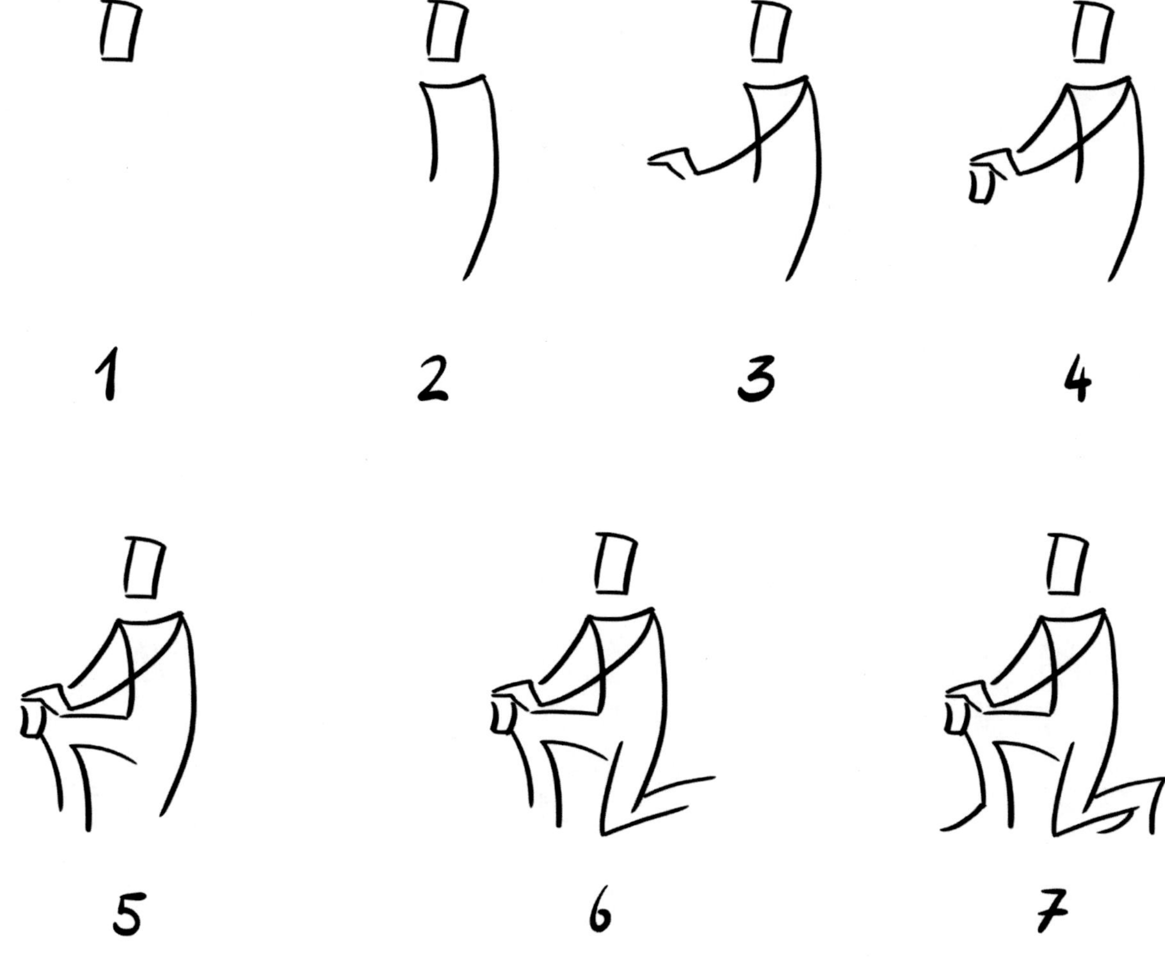
1
2
3
4
5
6
7

DAY 34

Doing the splits

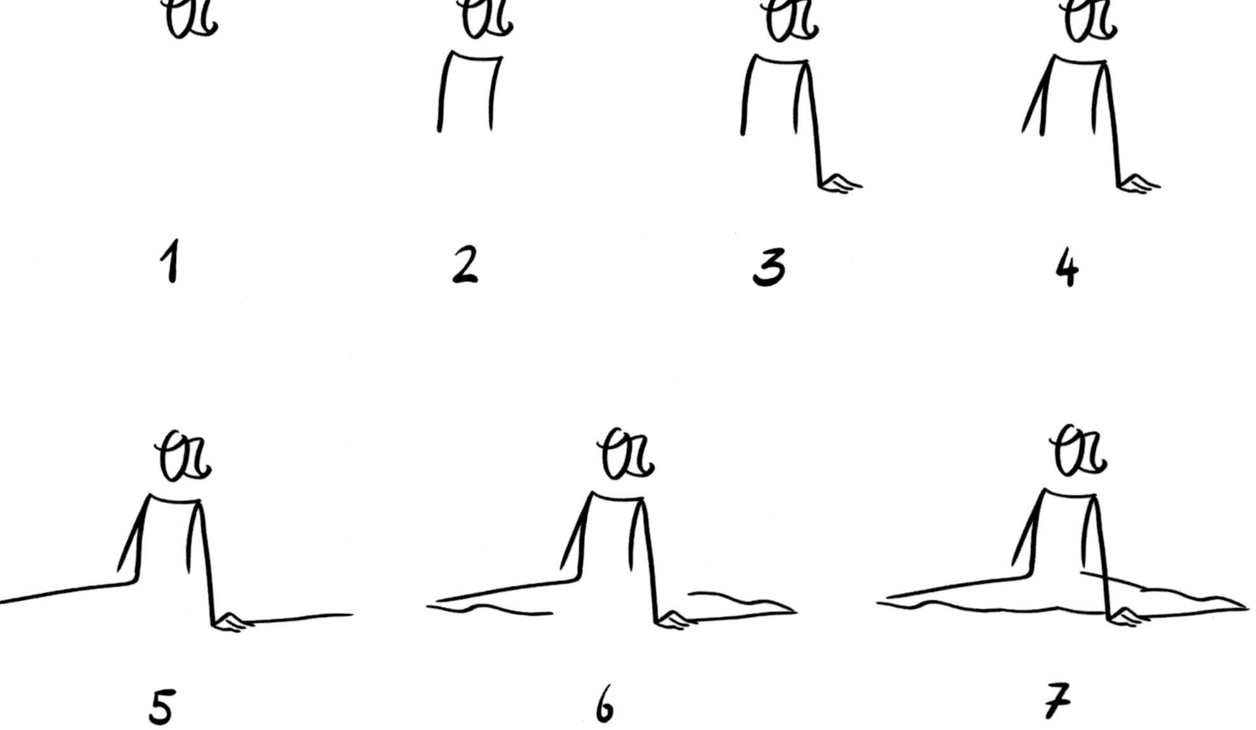
1
2
3
4
5
6
7

DAY 35

Doing a bridge pose

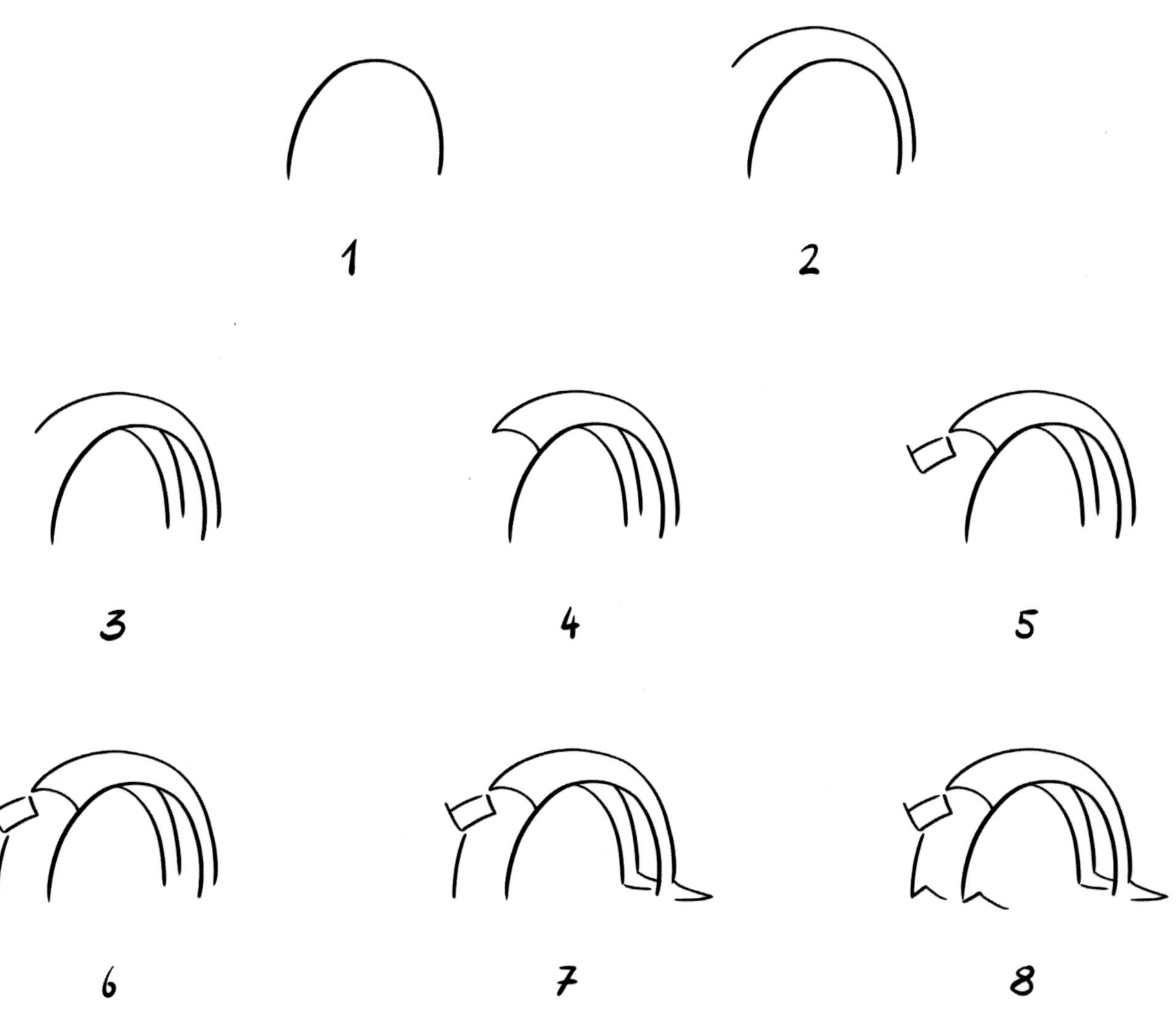

1
2
3
4
5
6
7
8

DAY 36

Kicking a stone

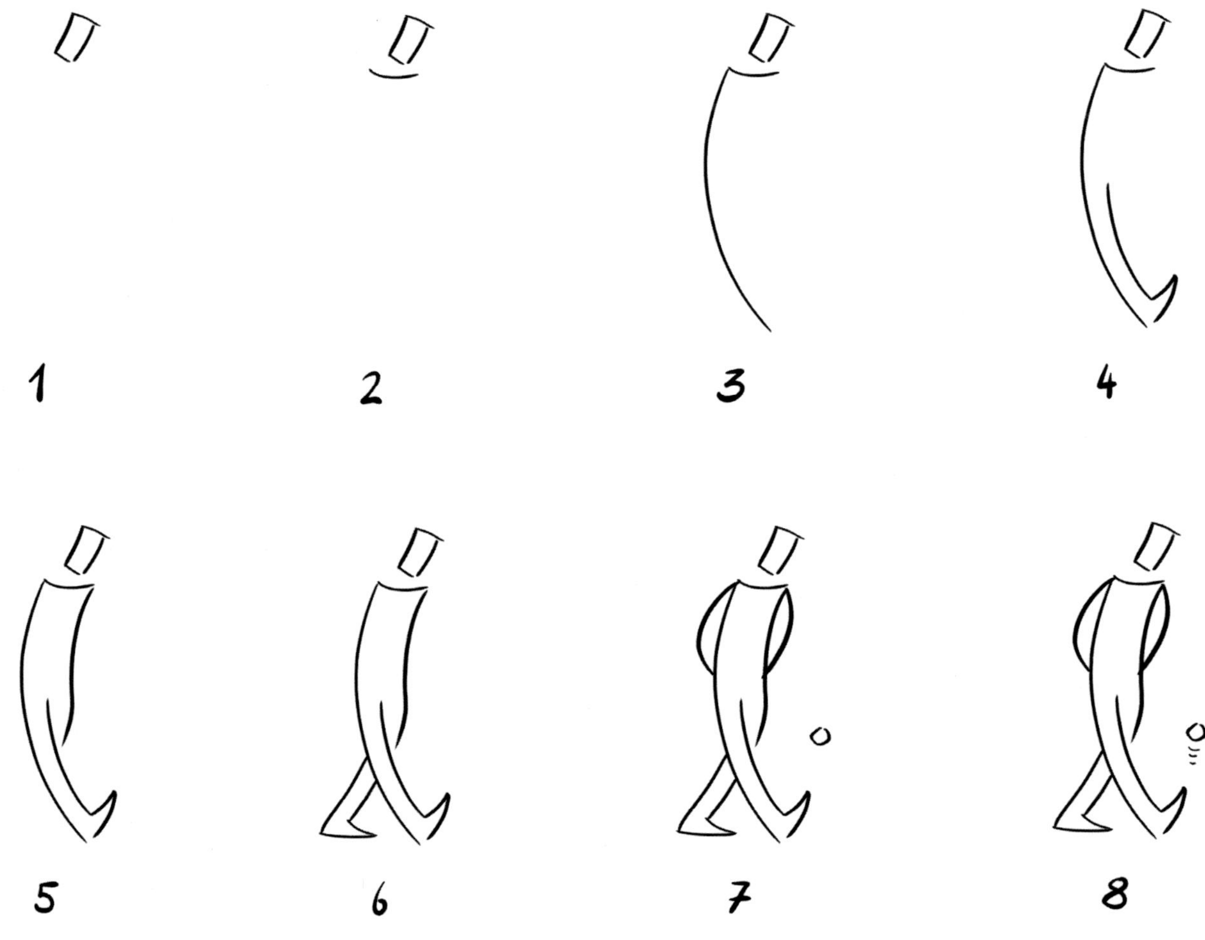

1
2
3
4
5
6
7
8

DAY 37

Throwing

1

2

3

4

5

6

7

8

DAY 38

Stretching

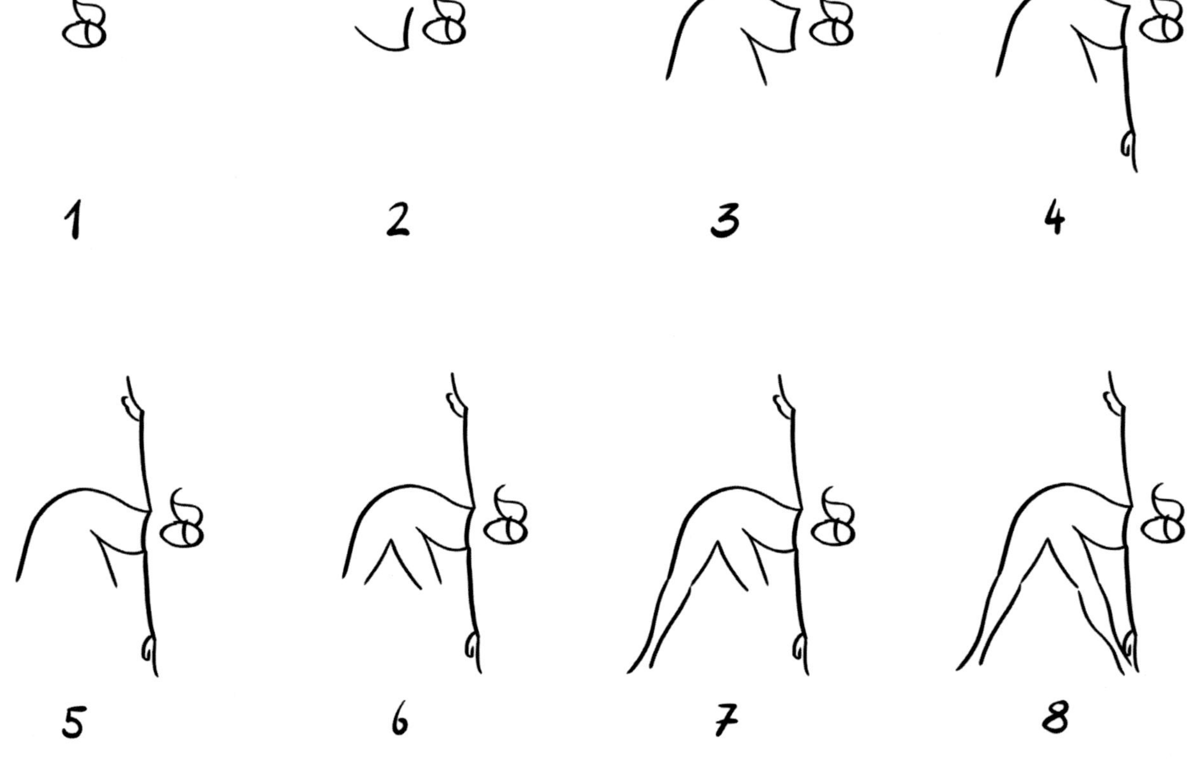
1
2
3
4
5
6
7
8

DAY 39

Doing push ups

1
2
3
4
5
6
7

DAY 40

Hiding behind a curtain

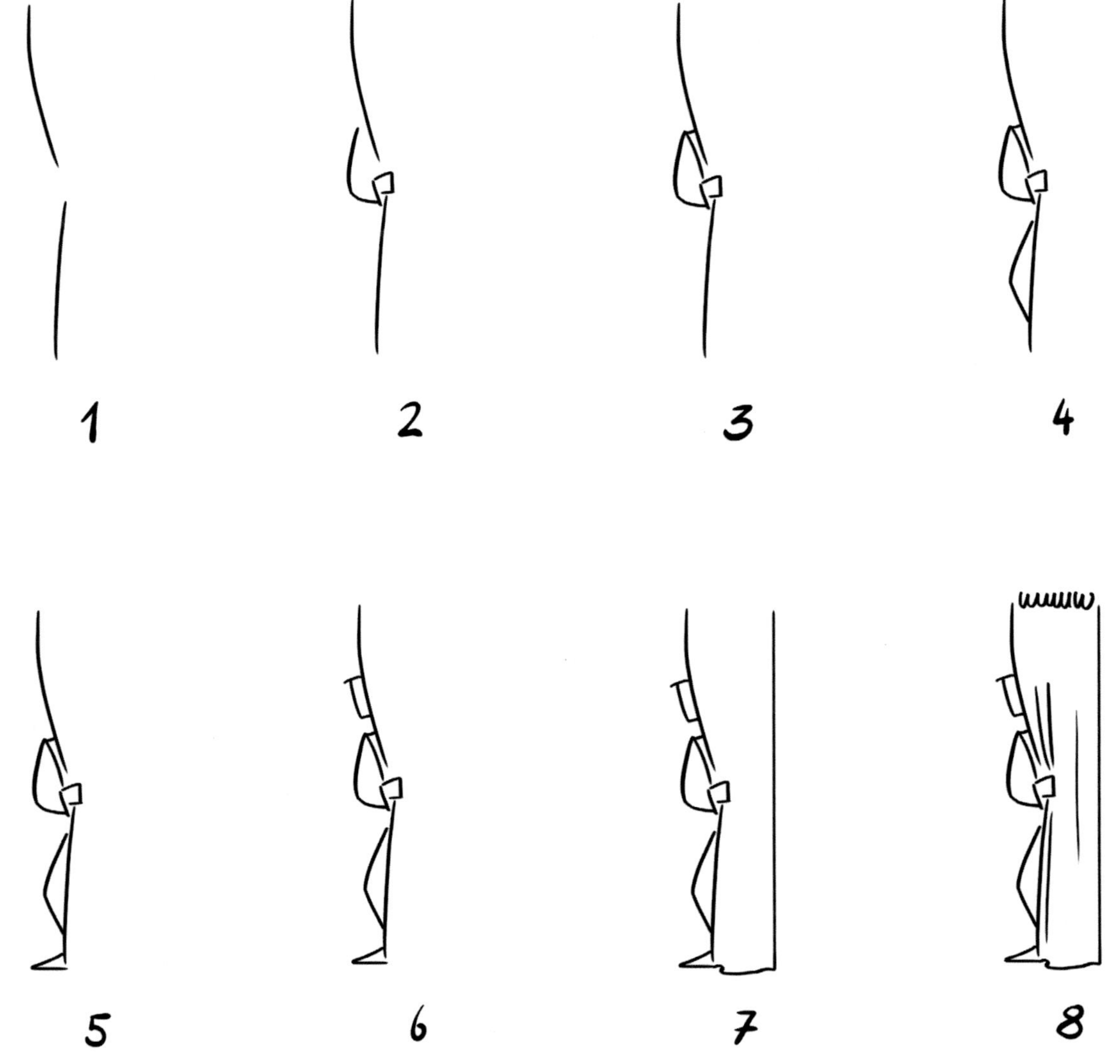

1
2
3
4
5
6
7
8

DAY 41

Waving a flag

1 2 3 4

5 6 7 8

DAY 42

Cupid

1
2
3
4
5
6
7
8

DAY 43

Crying

1 2 3 4

5 6 7 8

DAY 44

Crawling baby

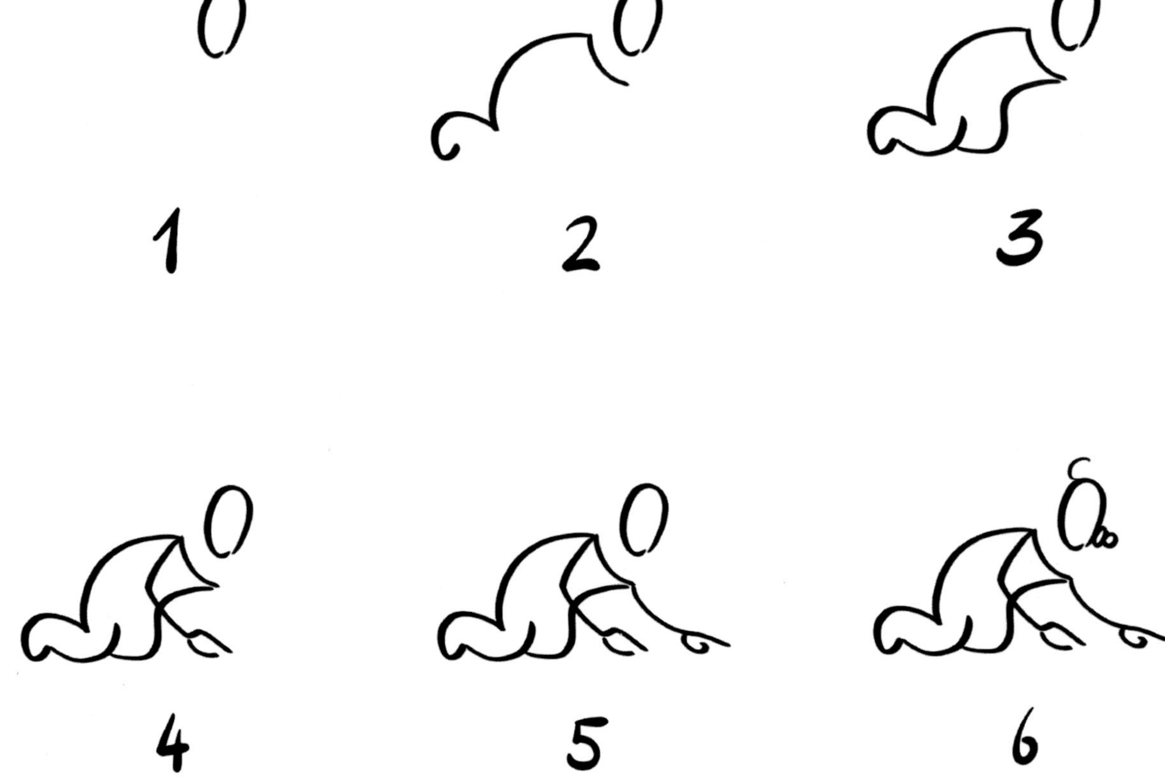

1
2
3
4
5
6

DAY 45

Baby making first steps

1

2

3

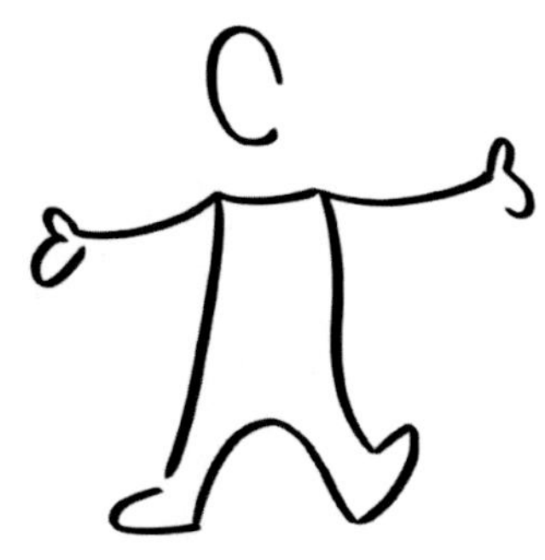

4

5

6

DAY 46

Falling

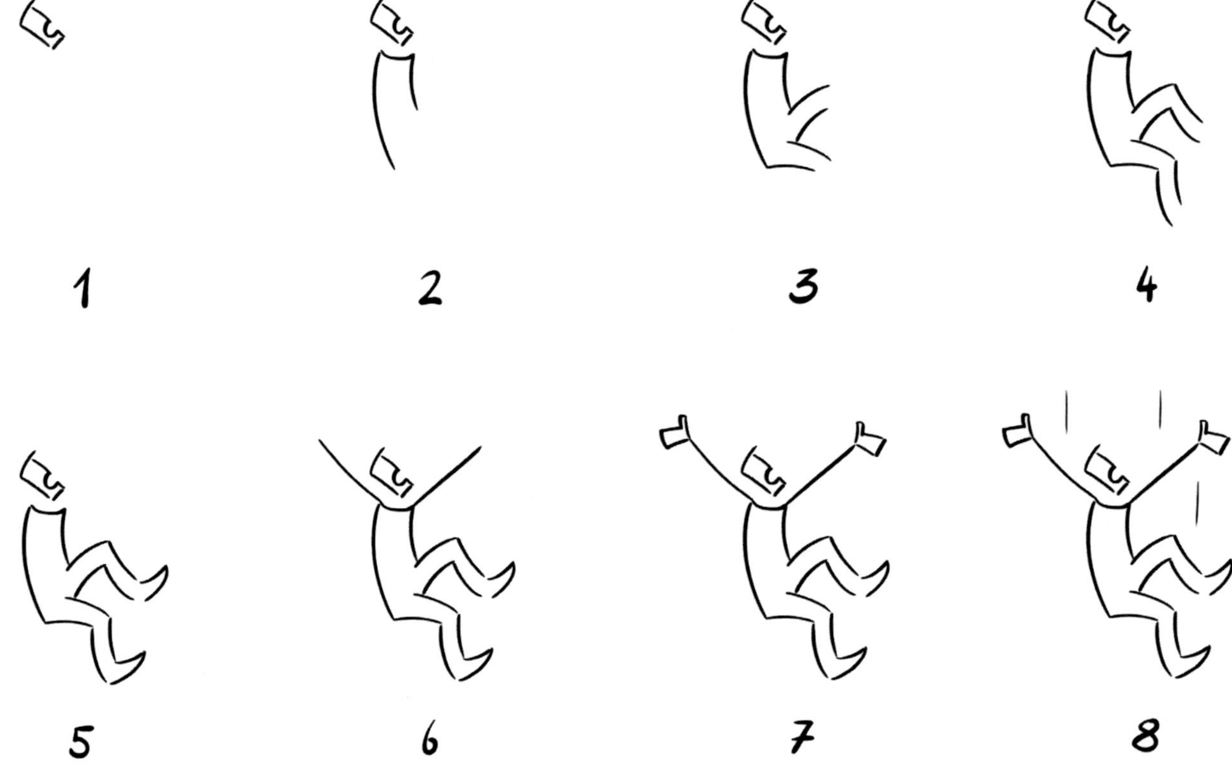

1
2
3
4
5
6
7
8

DAY 47

Jumping a hurdle

1 2 3 4

5 6 7 8

DAY 48

Sisyphos

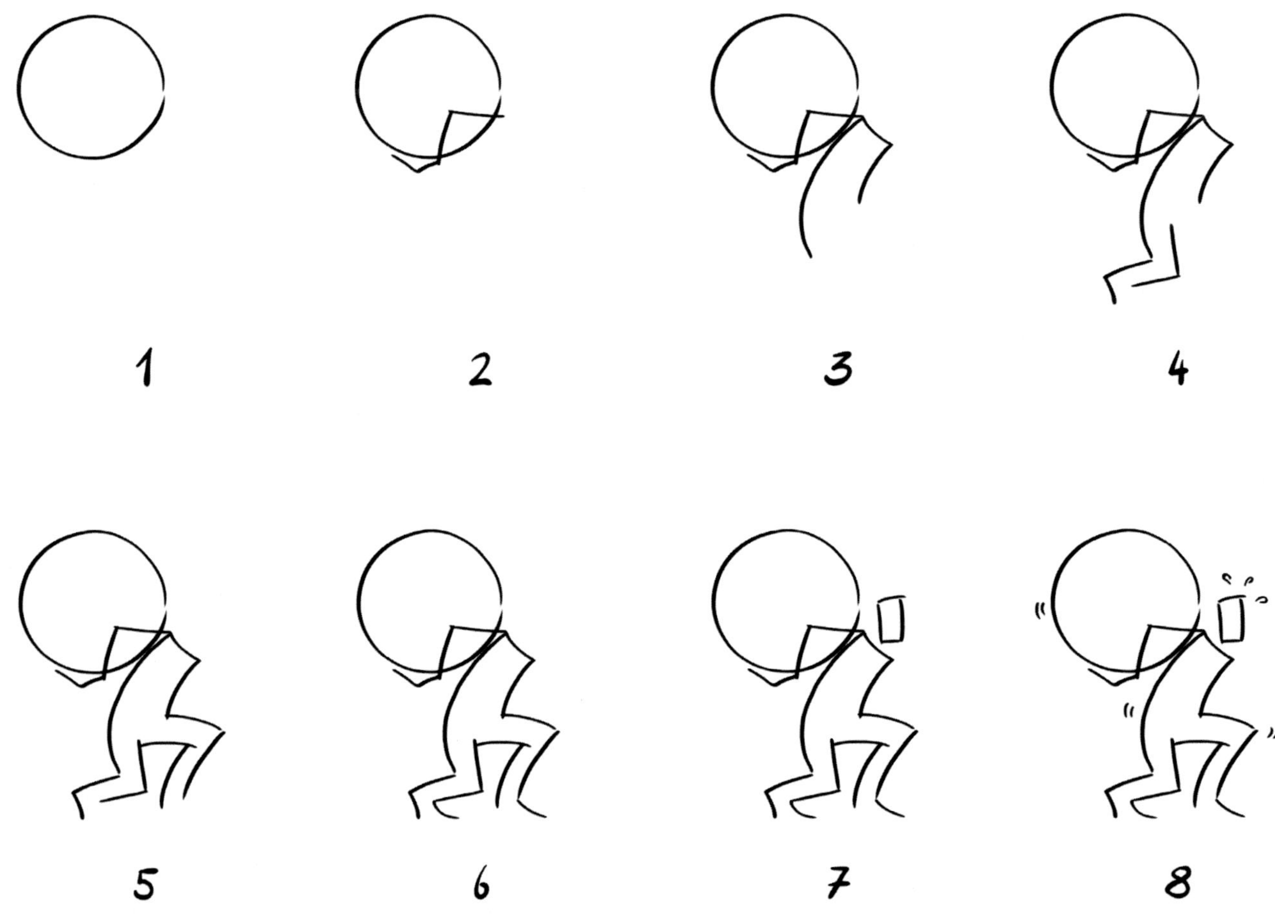
1
2
3
4
5
6
7
8

Stopping suddenly

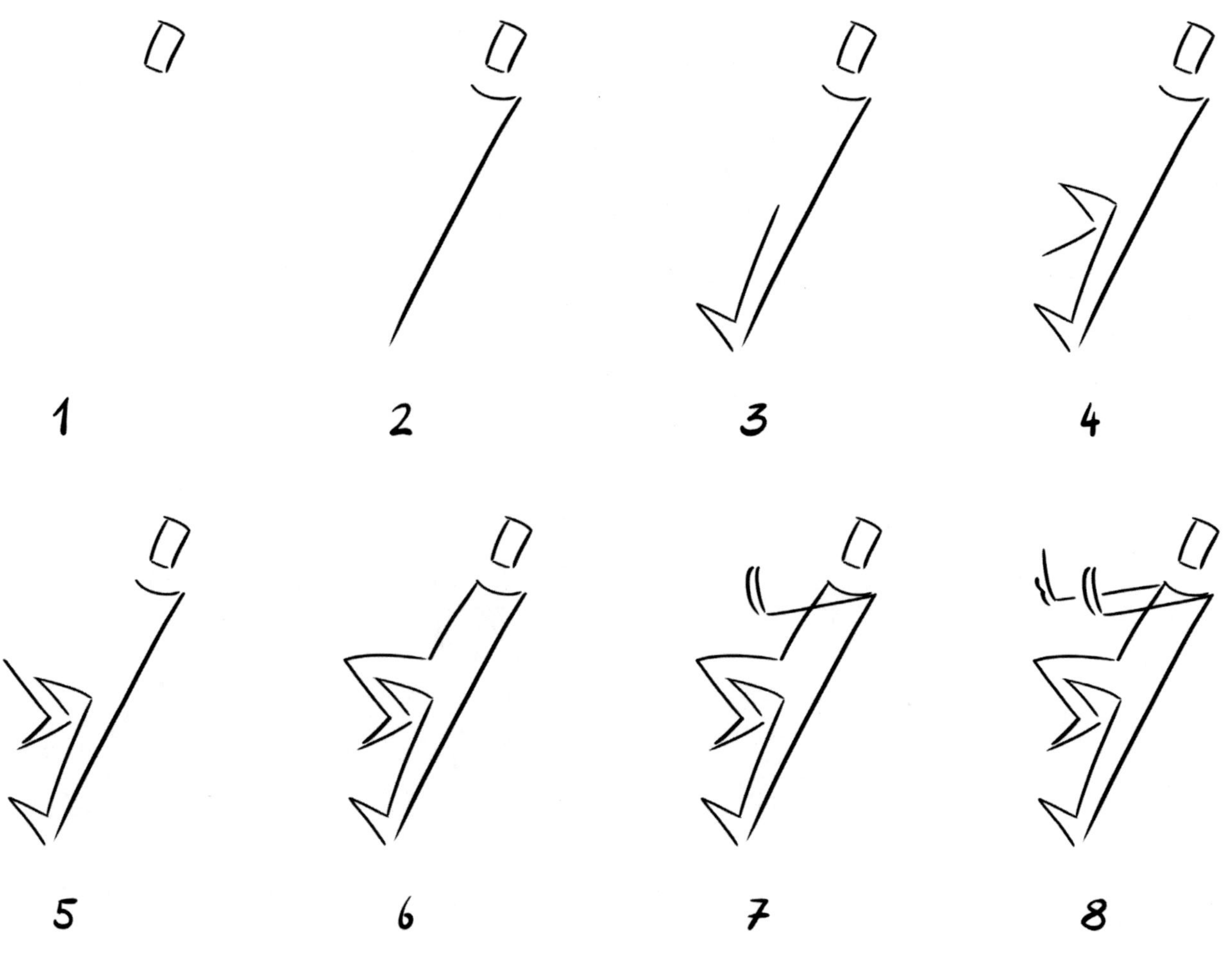
1
2
3
4
5
6
7
8

DAY 50

Using a walking stick

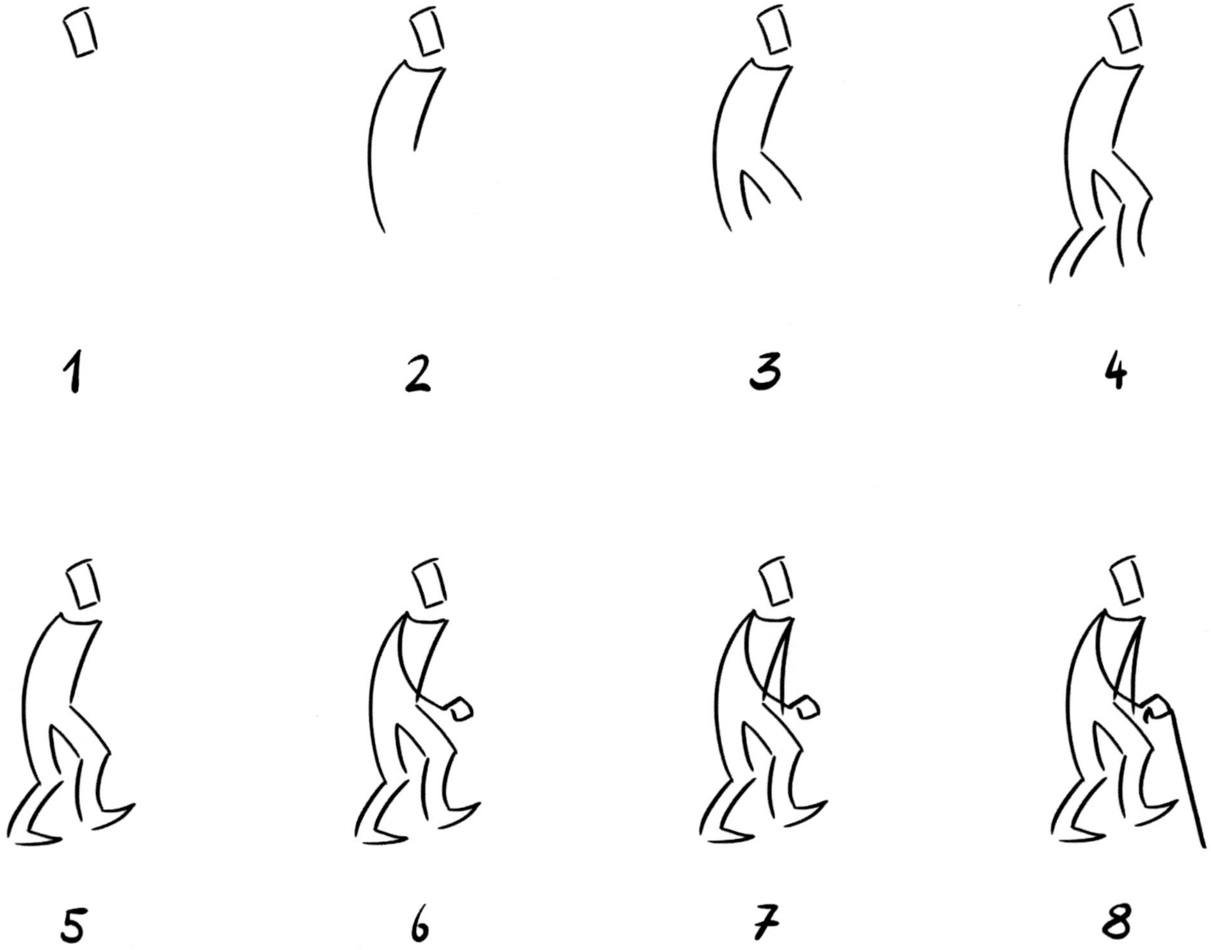

1 2 3 4

5 6 7 8

DAY 51

Travelling

1

2

3

4

5

6

7

8

DAY 52

Slam dunk

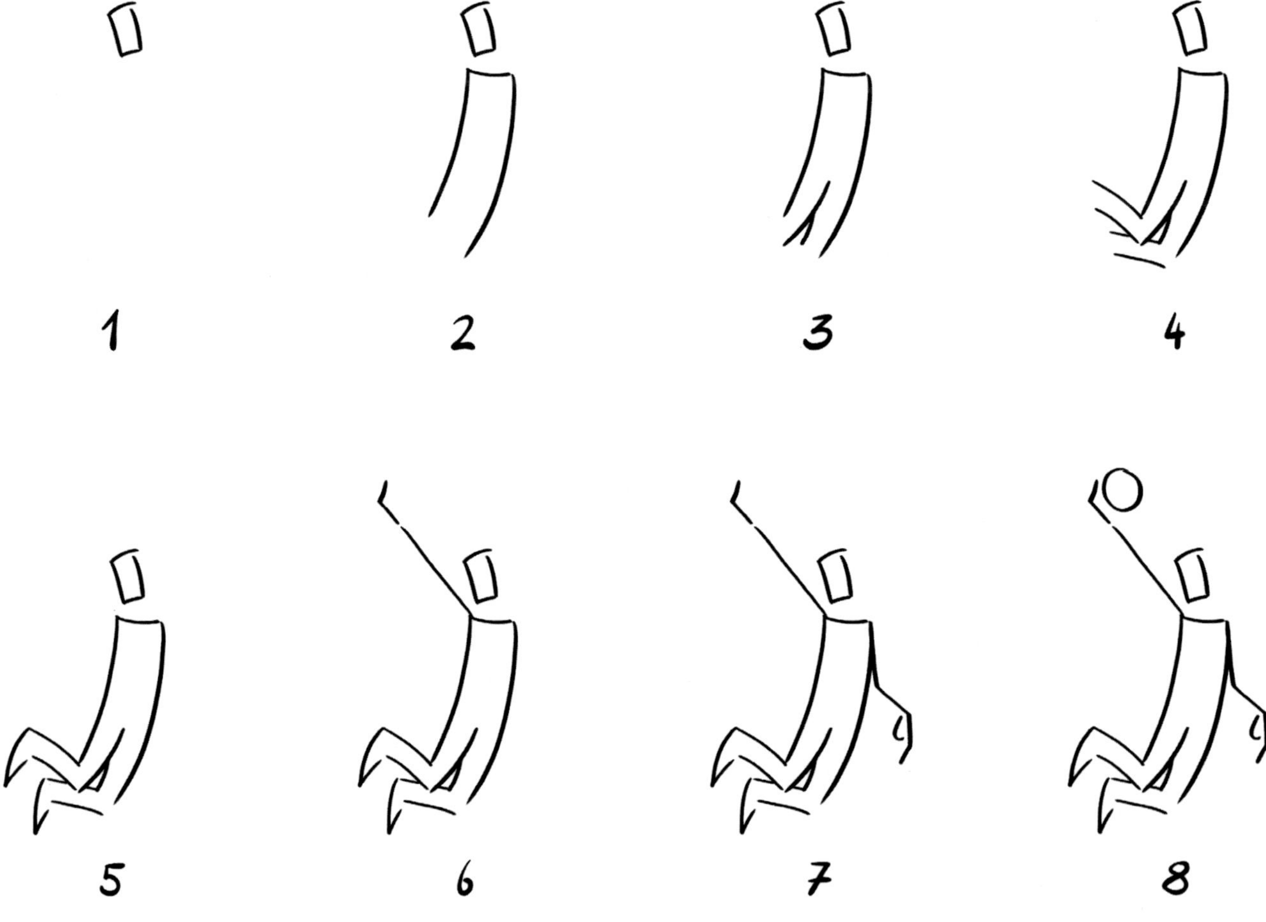
1
2
3
4
5
6
7
8

DAY 53

Practicing karate

1 2 3

4

5

6

DAY 54

Bowling

1
2
3
4
5
6
7
8

DAY 55

Cleaning

1 2 3 4

5 6 7 8

DAY 56

Stomping

1
2
3
4

5 6 7 8

DAY 57

Sitting thinking

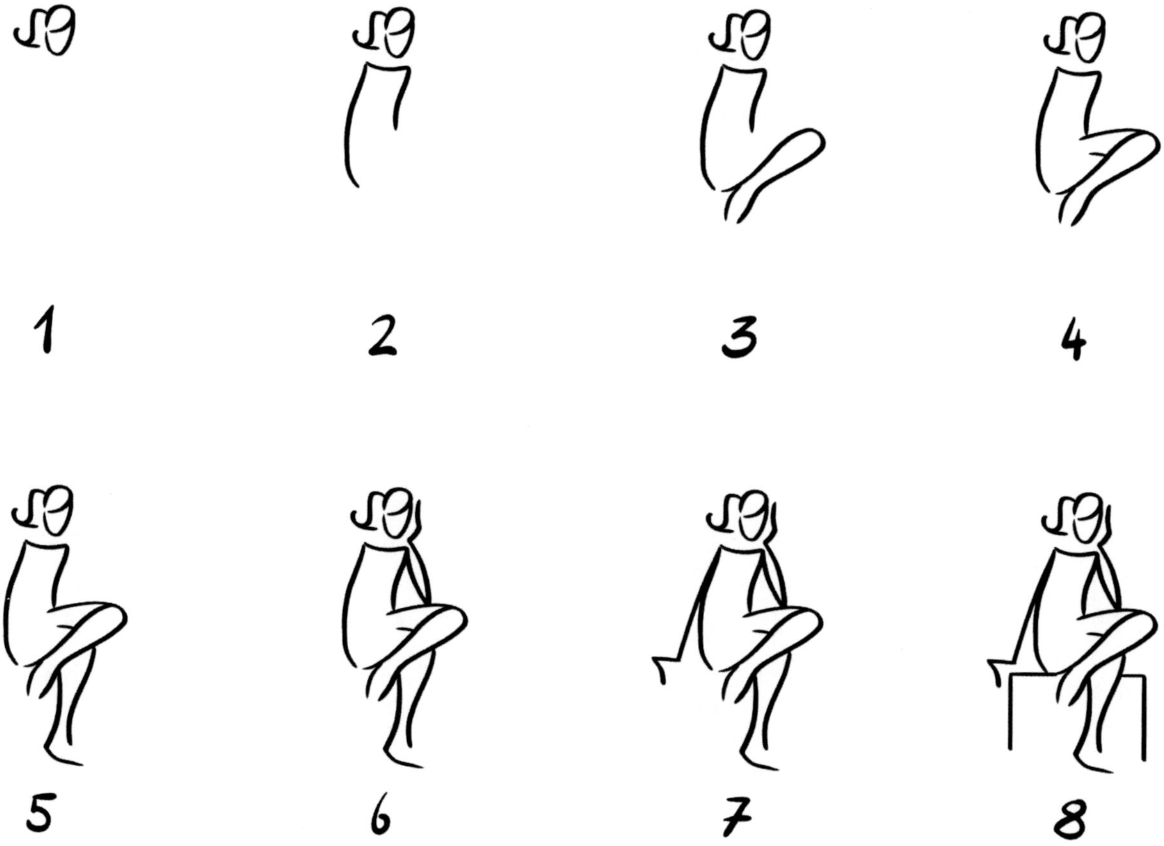

1

2

3

4

5

6

7

8

DAY 58

Trusting

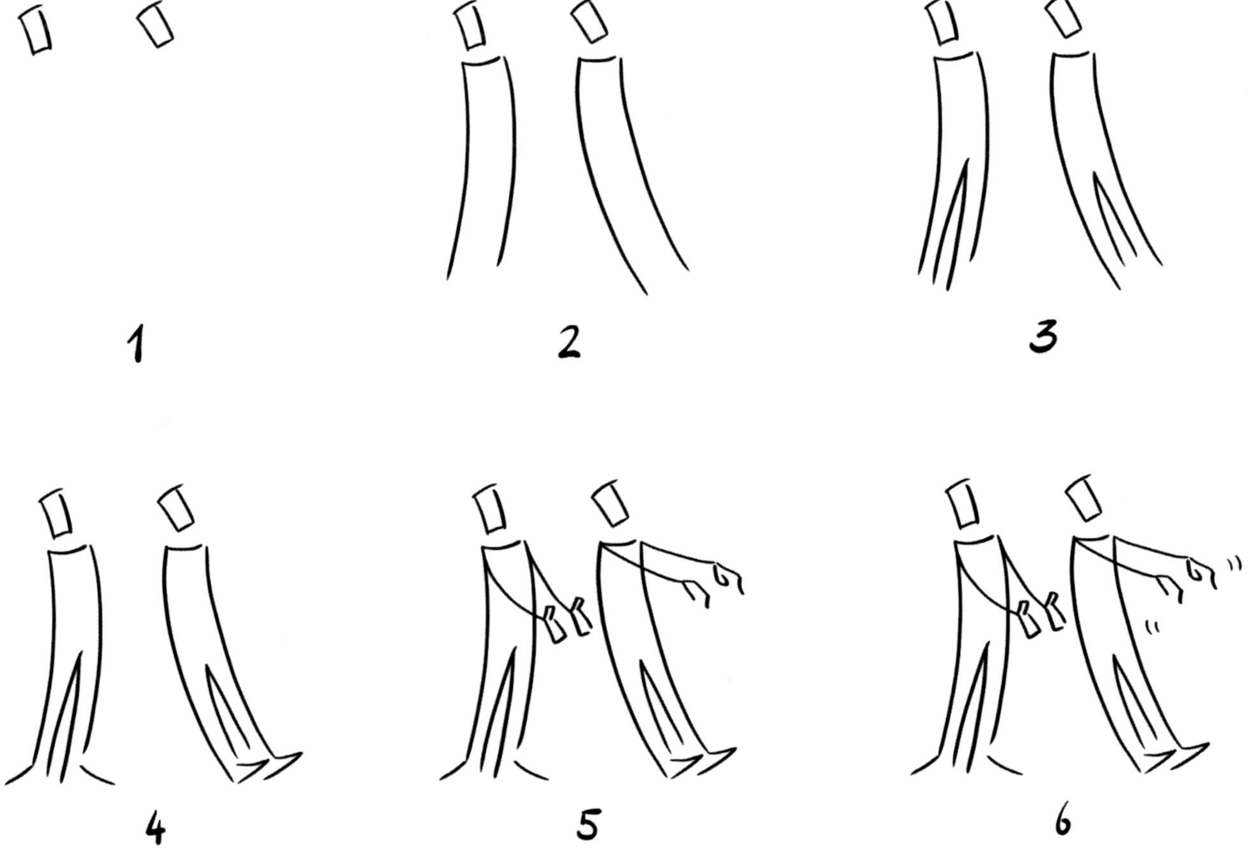
1
2
3
4
5
6

DAY 59

Wielding a pickaxe

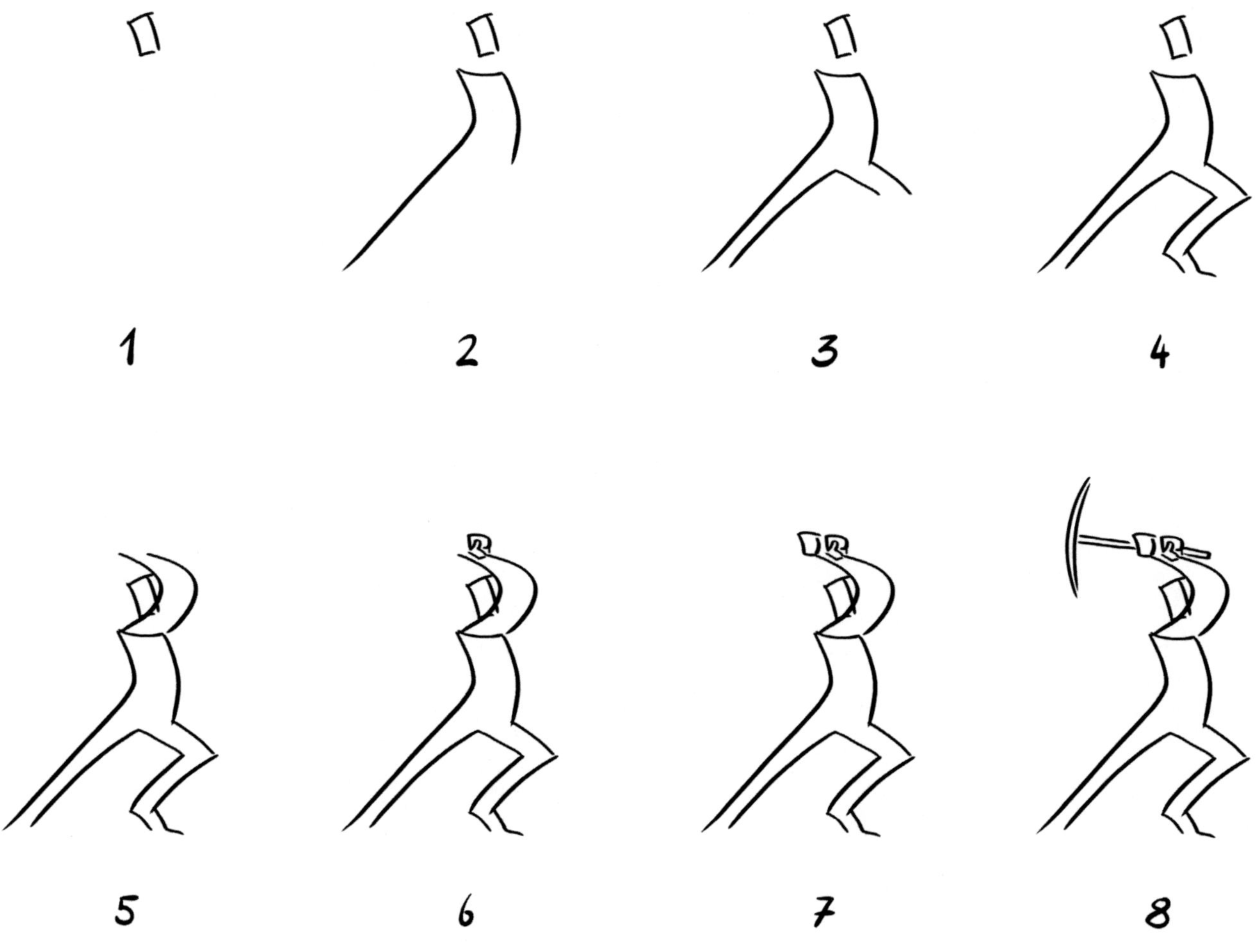

1
2
3
4
5
6
7
8

Painting

1

2

3

4

5

6

7

8

DAY 61

Using a camera

1

2

3

4

5

6

7

8

DAY 62

Rocking at a concert

1

2

3

4

5

6

7

8

DAY 63

Kazachok dancing

1

2

3

4

5

6

7

DAY 64

Breakdancing

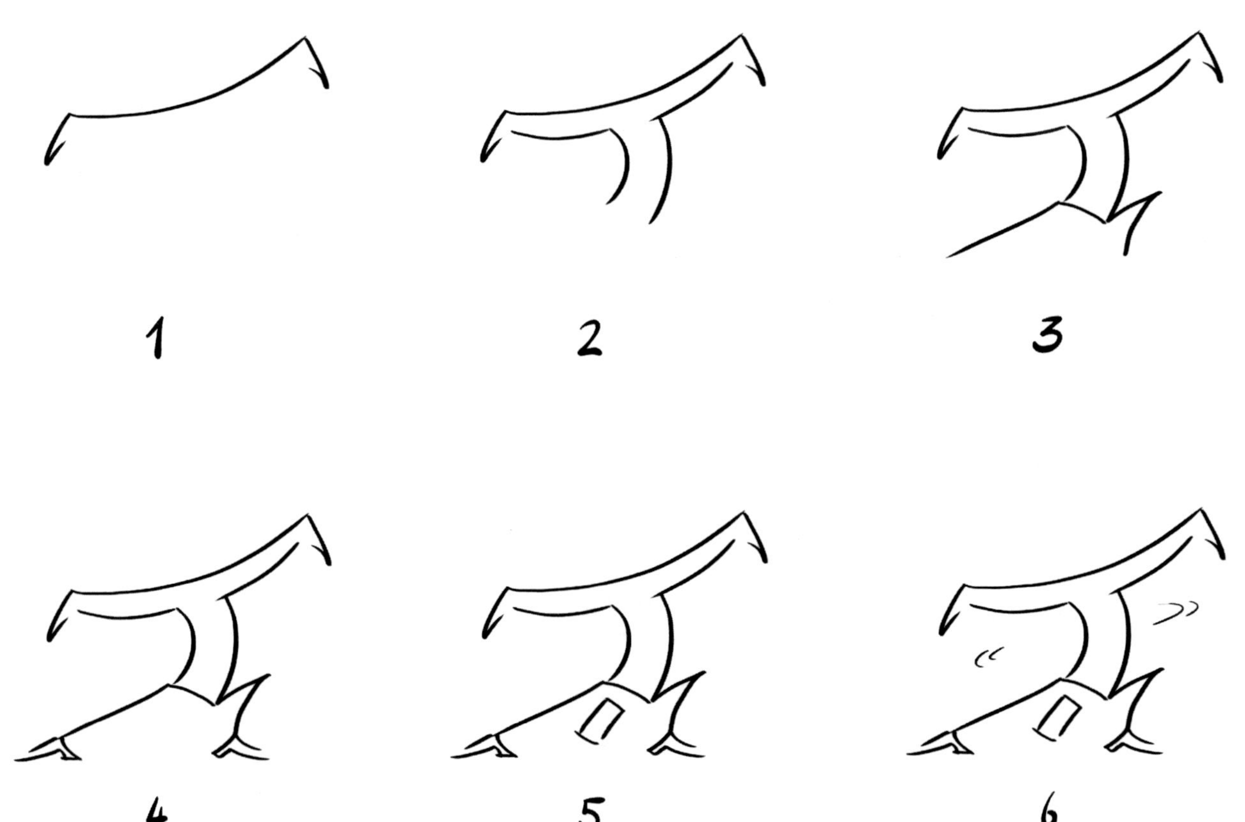

1
2
3
4
5
6

DAY 65

Ballet dancing

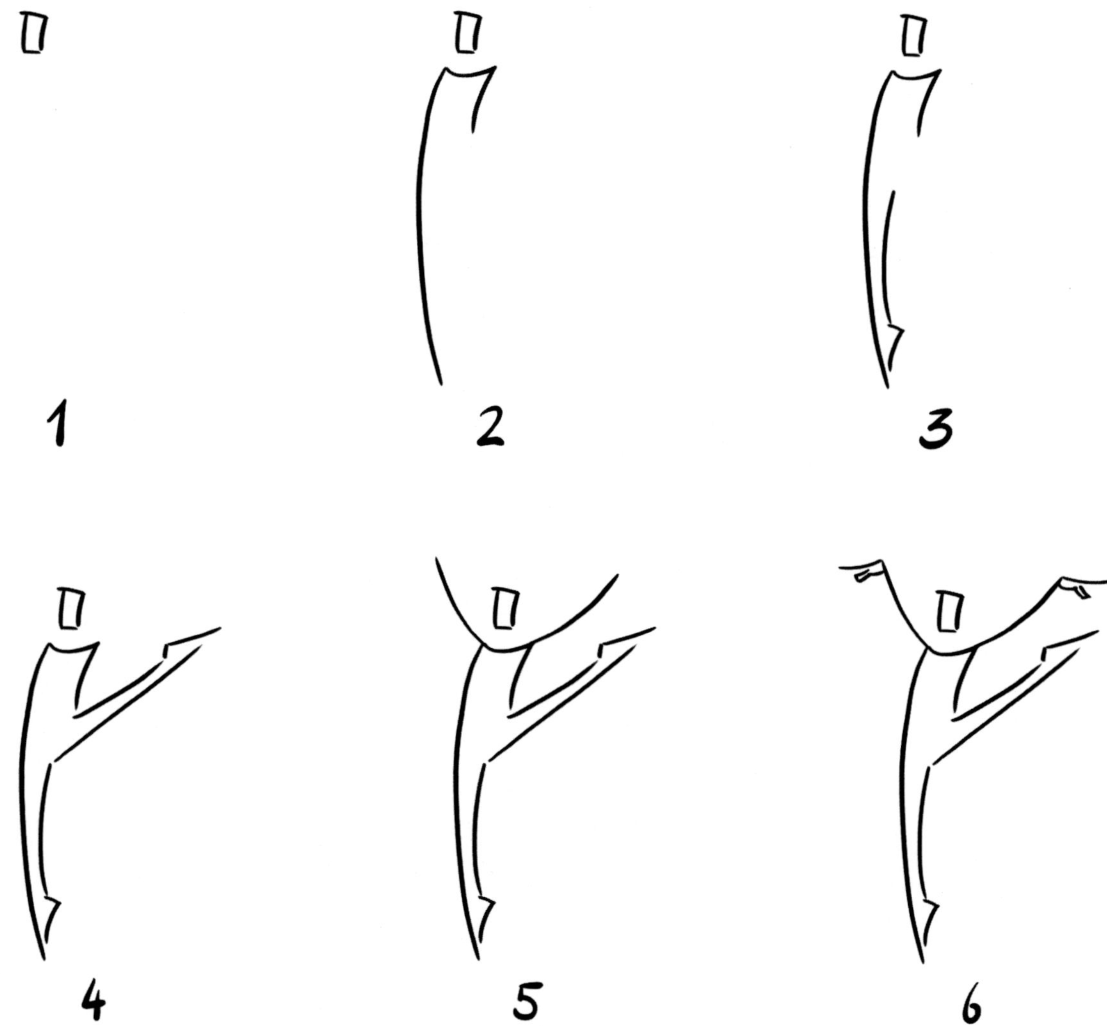

1
2
3
4
5
6

DAY 66

Curtsying

1 2 3 4

5 6 7 8

DAY 67

Bowing

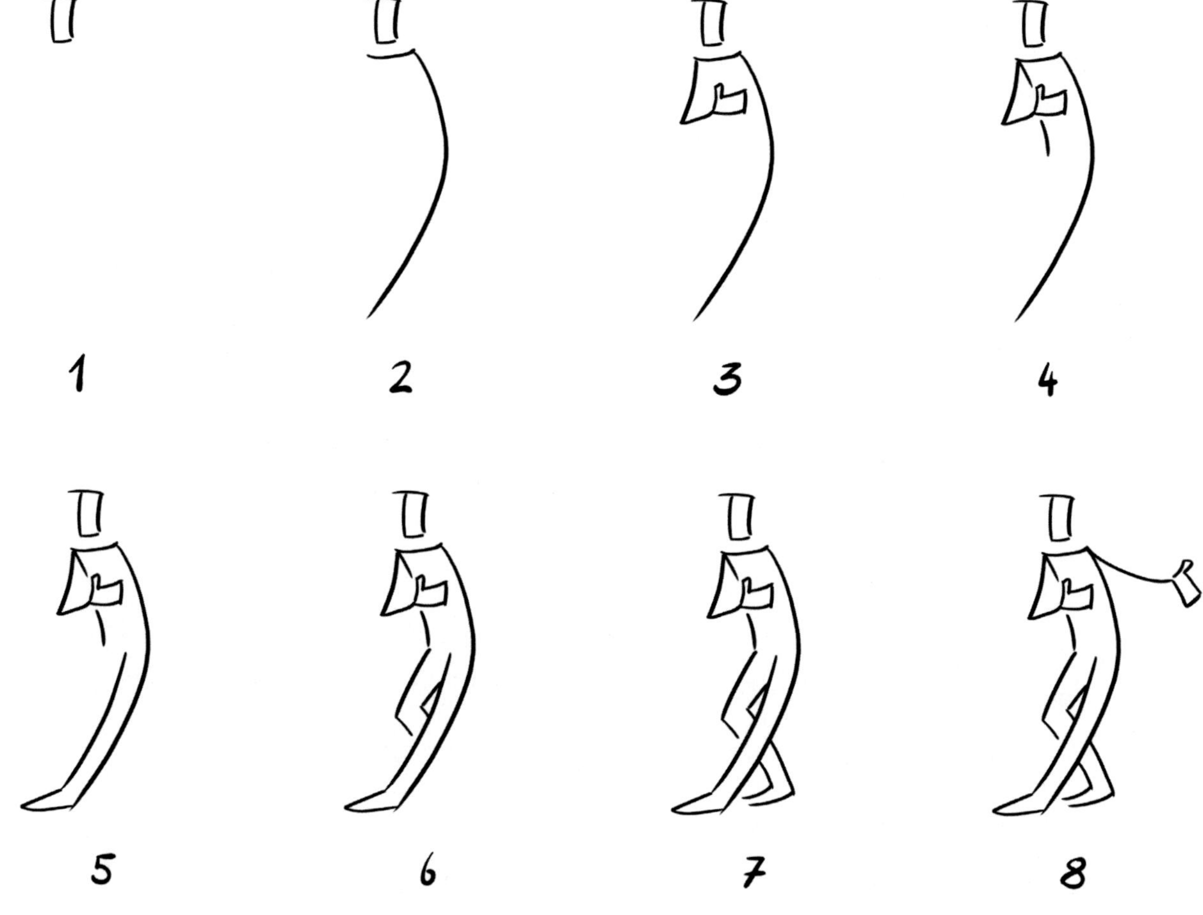

1
2
3
4
5
6
7
8

DAY 68

Doing a salto

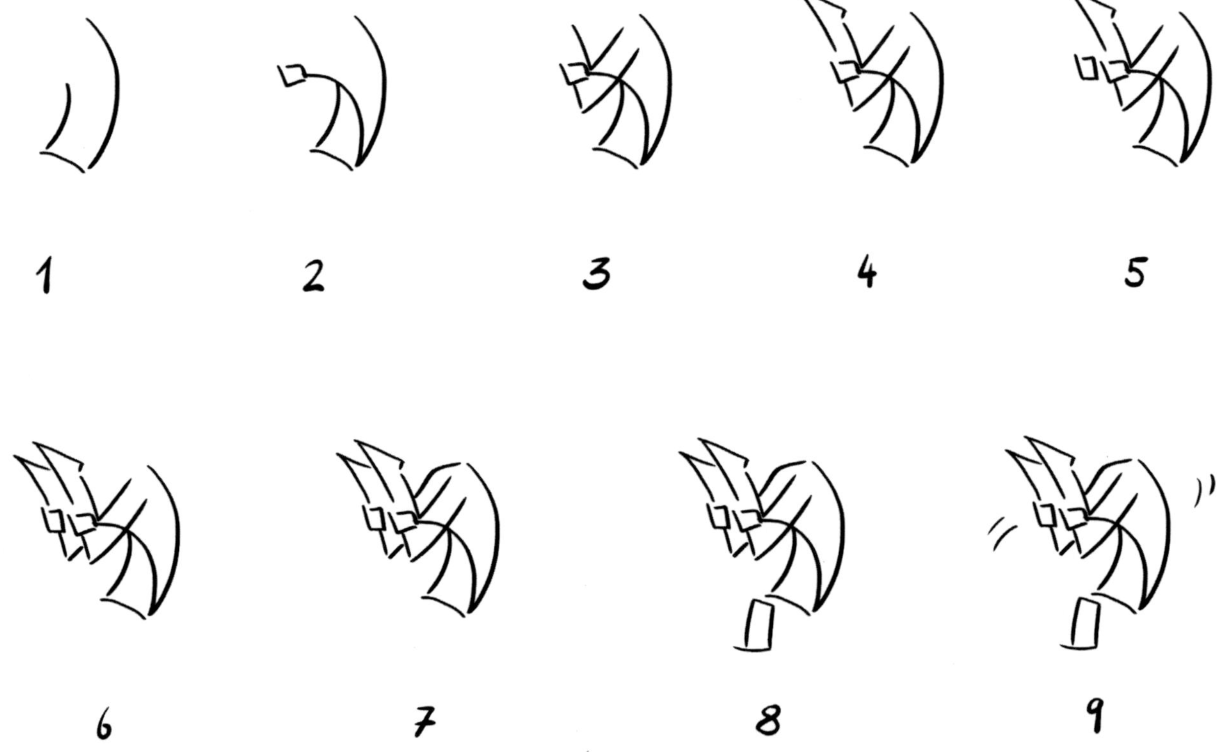

1
2
3
4
5
6
7
8
9

DAY 69

Skateboarding

1
2
3
4
5
6
7
8
9

DAY 70

Climbing a rope

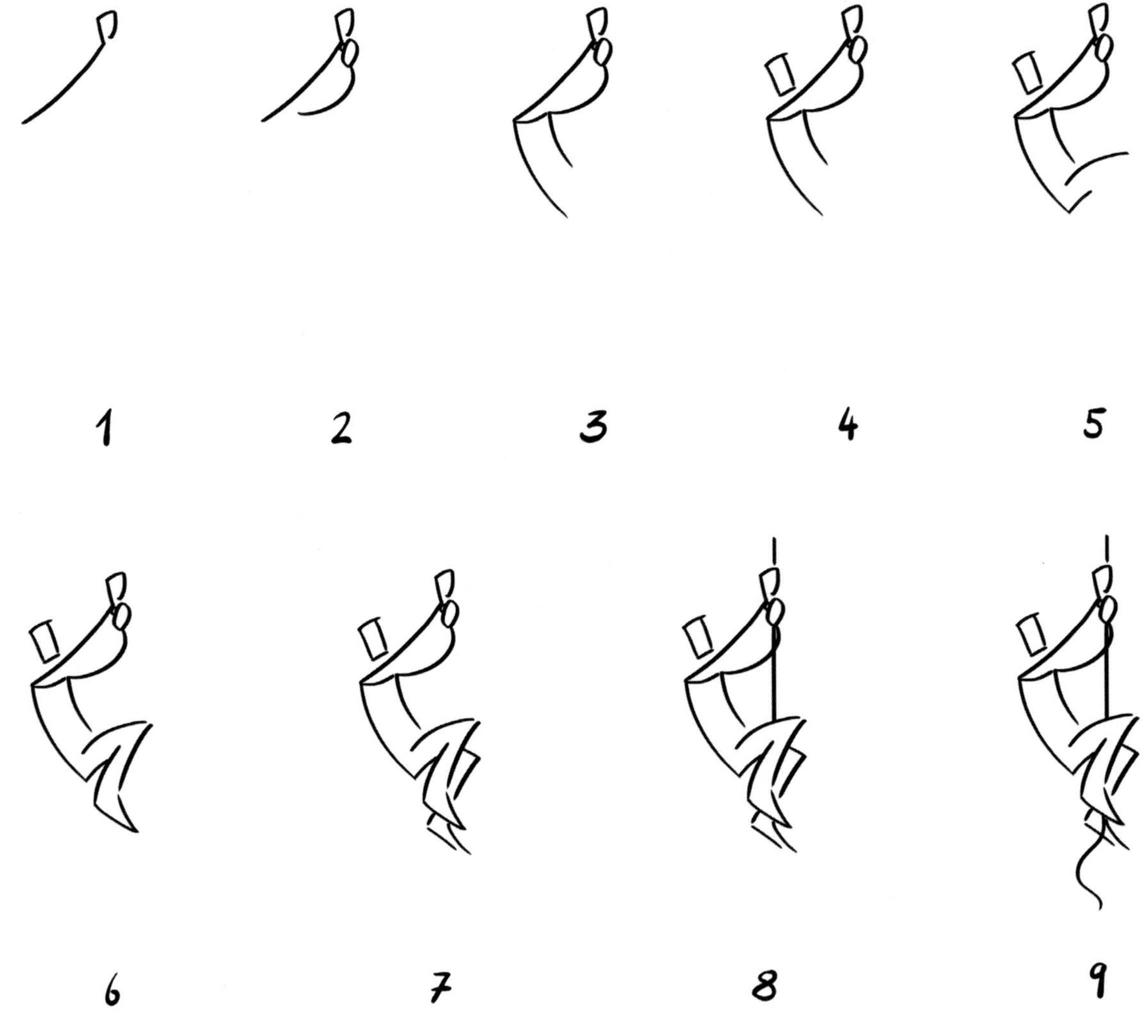

1
2
3
4
5
6
7
8
9

DAY 71

Pushing

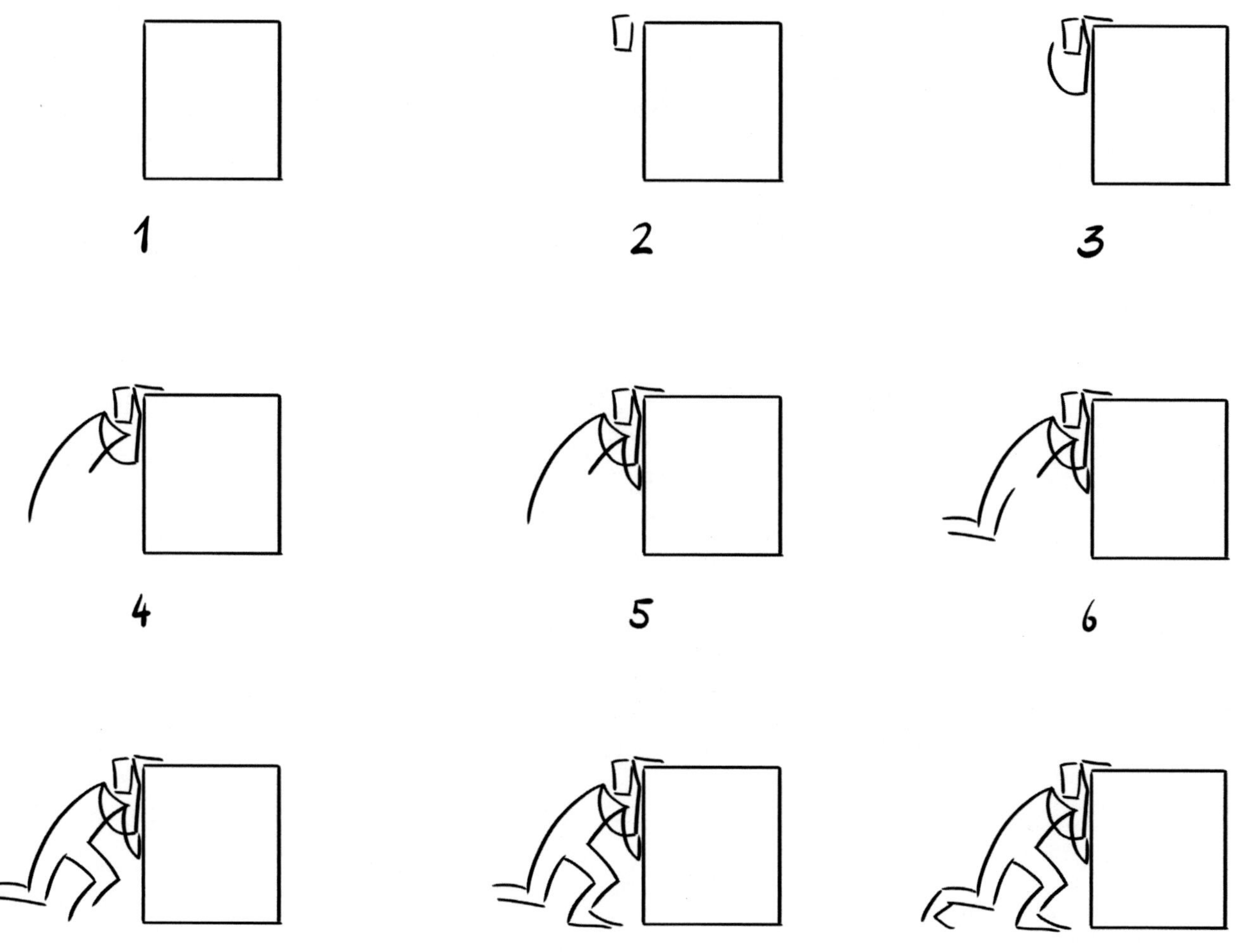

1
2
3
4
5
6
7
8
9

DAY 72

Drinking

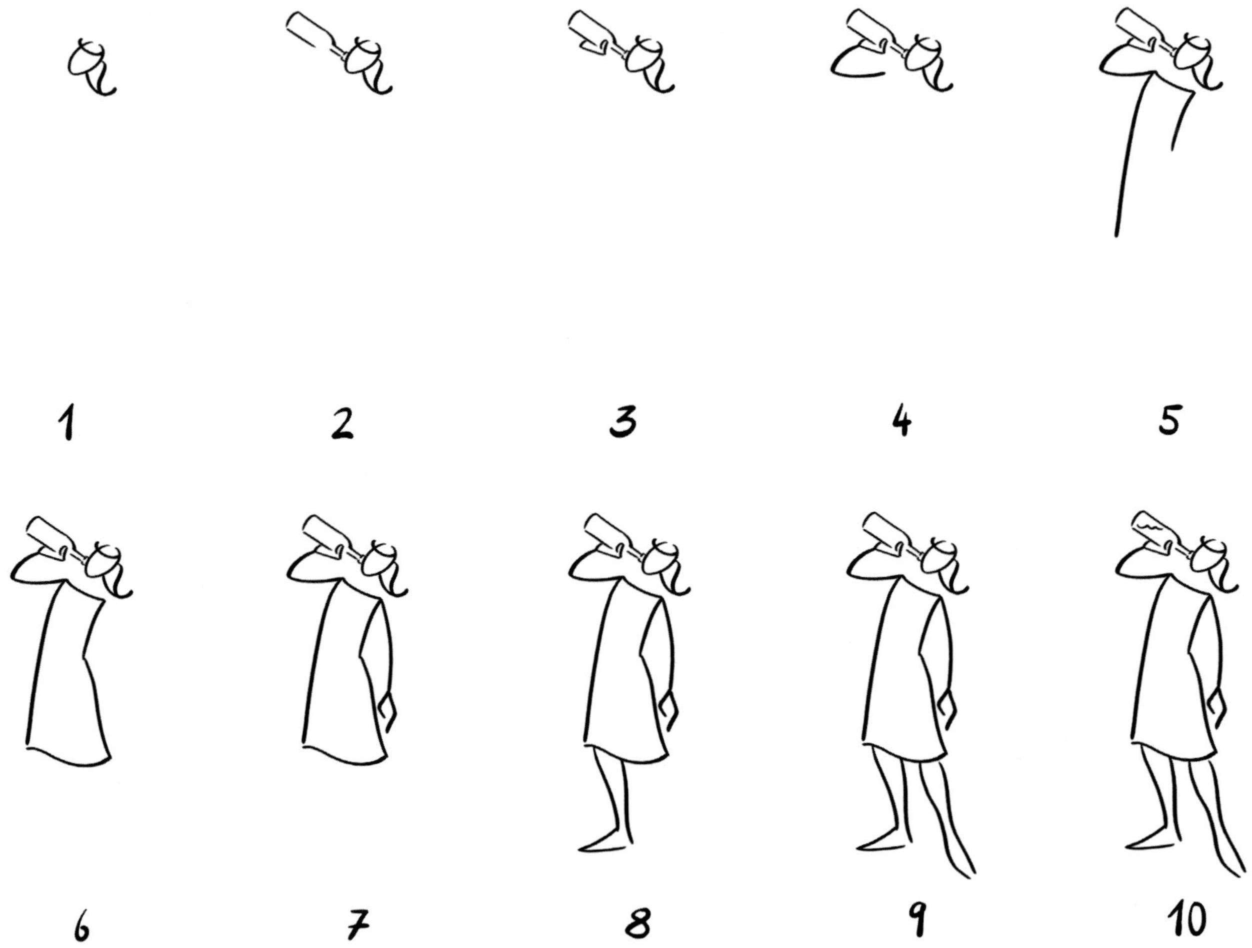

1 2 3 4 5

6 7 8 9 10

DAY 73

Playing billiards

1
2
3
4
5
6
7
8
9

DAY 74

Taking high heel shoes off

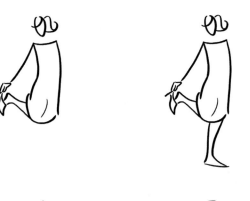

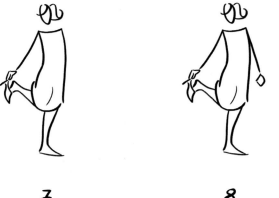

1 2 3 4 5

6 7 8 9

DAY 75

Tieing shoes

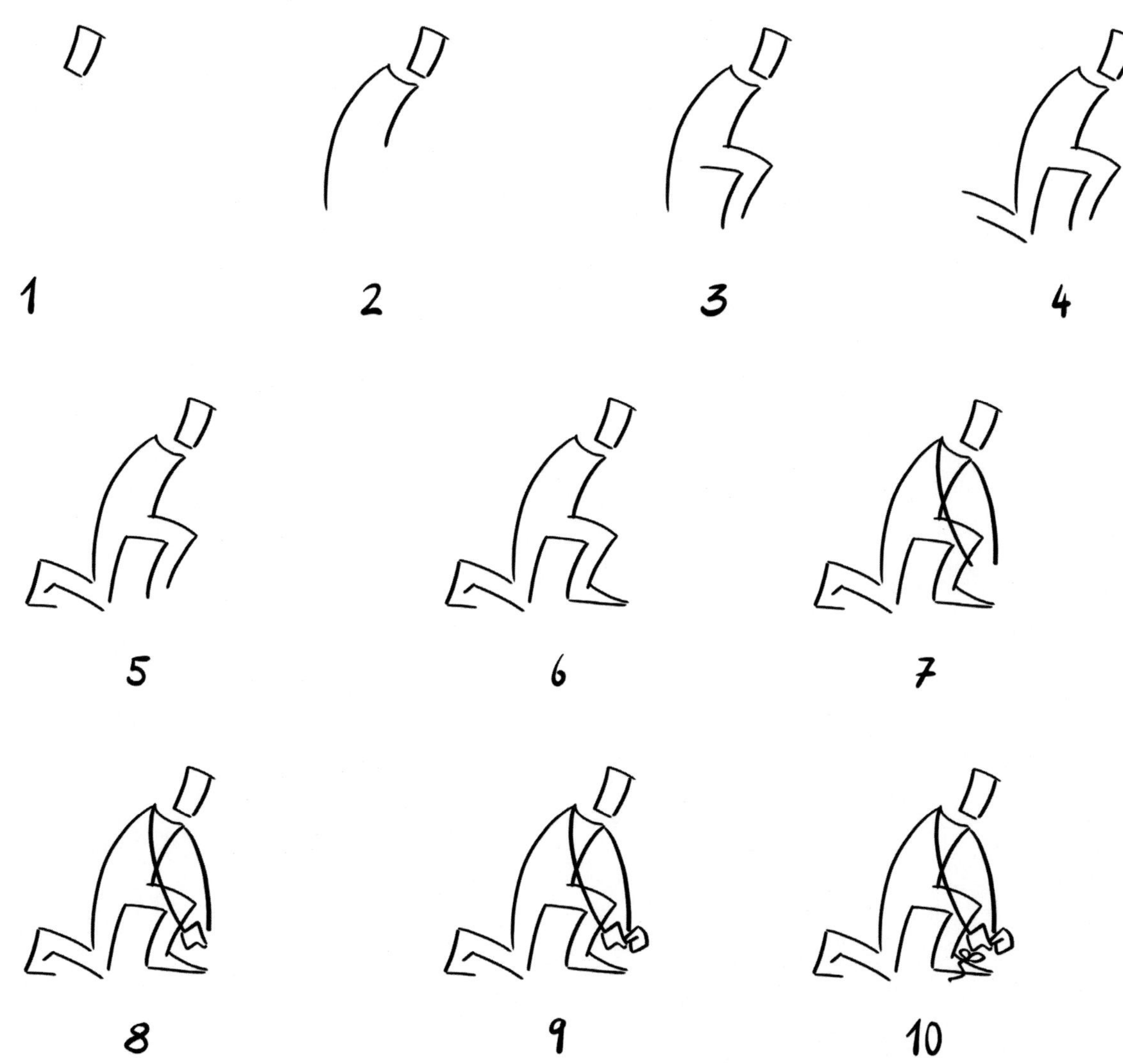

1
2
3
4
5
6
7
8
9
10

DAY 76

Petting a cat

1 2 3 4 5

6 7 8 9

DAY 77

Clay sculpting

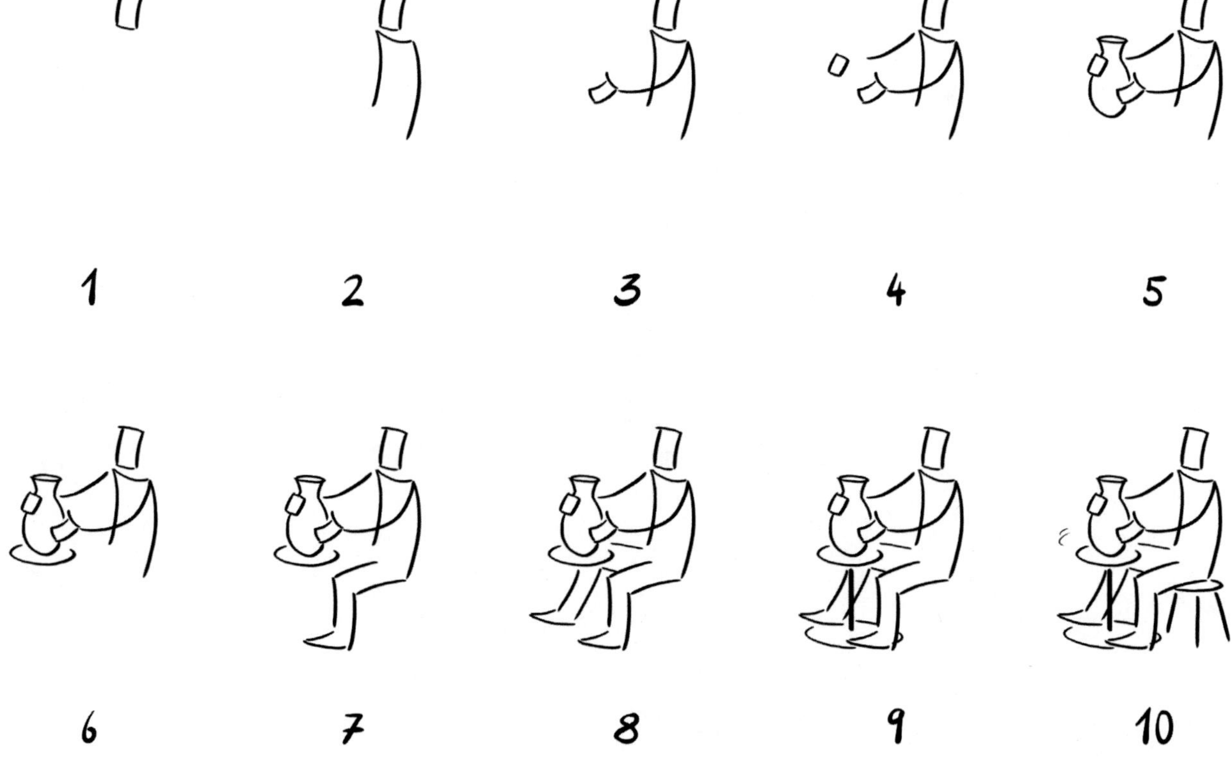

1
2
3
4
5
6
7
8
9
10

DAY 78

Boxing

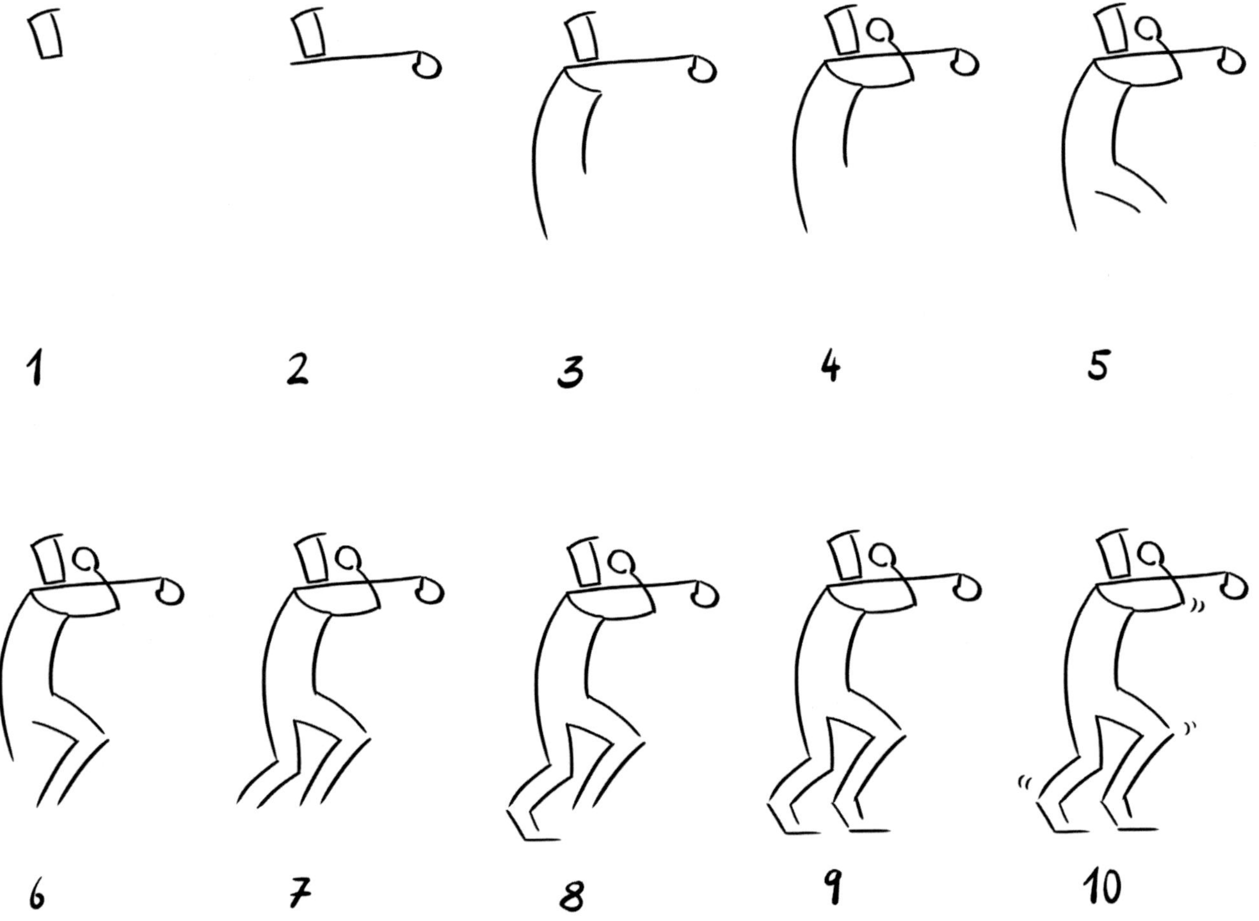

1
2
3
4
5
6
7
8
9
10

DAY 79

Swimming

1

2

3

4

5

6

7

8

9

DAY 80

Vitruvian man

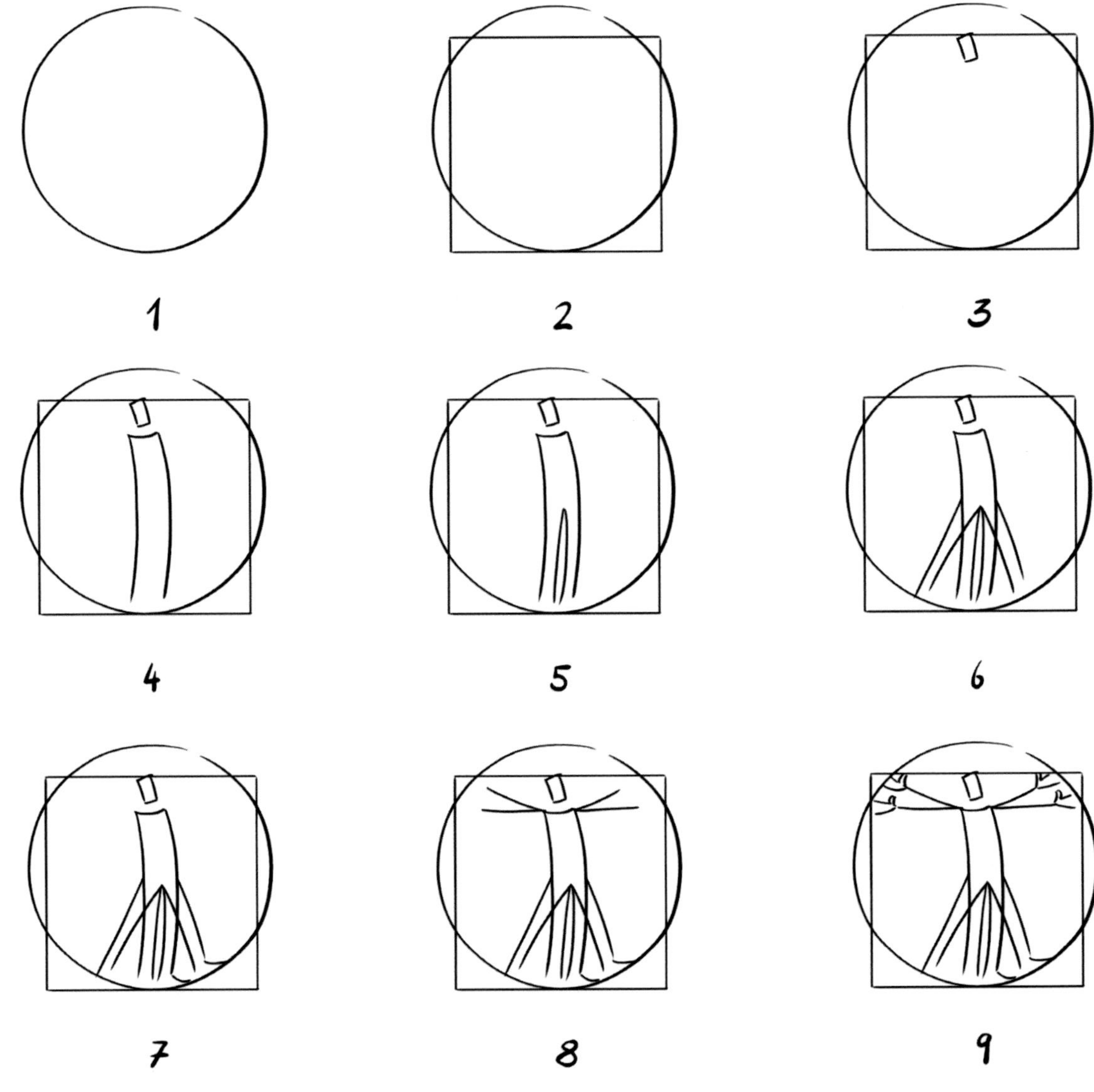
1
2
3
4
5
6
7
8
9

DAY 81

Astronaut

1
2
3
4
5
6
7
8
9

DAY 82

Waiting

1
2
3
4
5
6
7
8
9
10

DAY 83

Starting a race

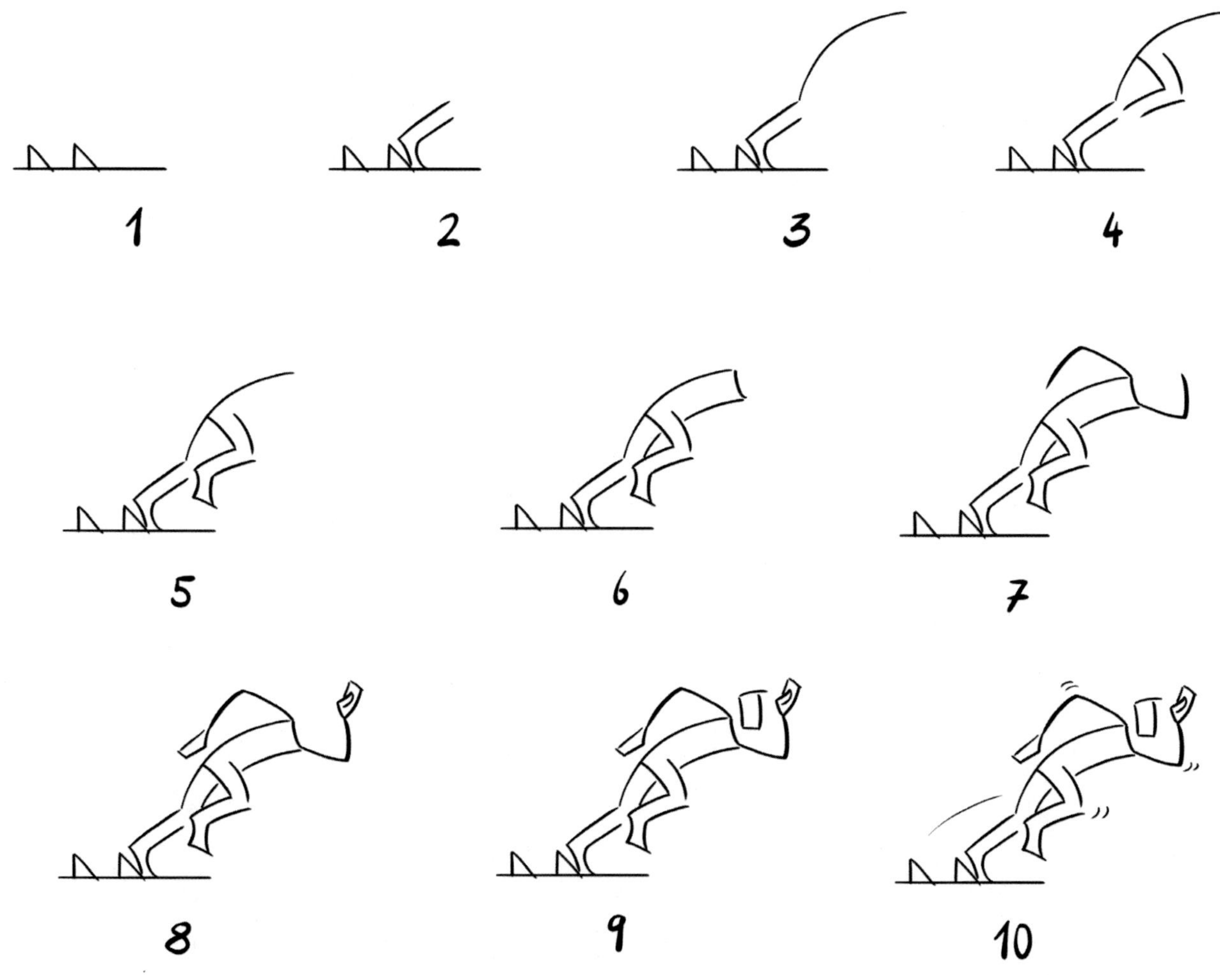
1
2
3
4
5
6
7
8
9
10

DAY 84

Walking a dachsund

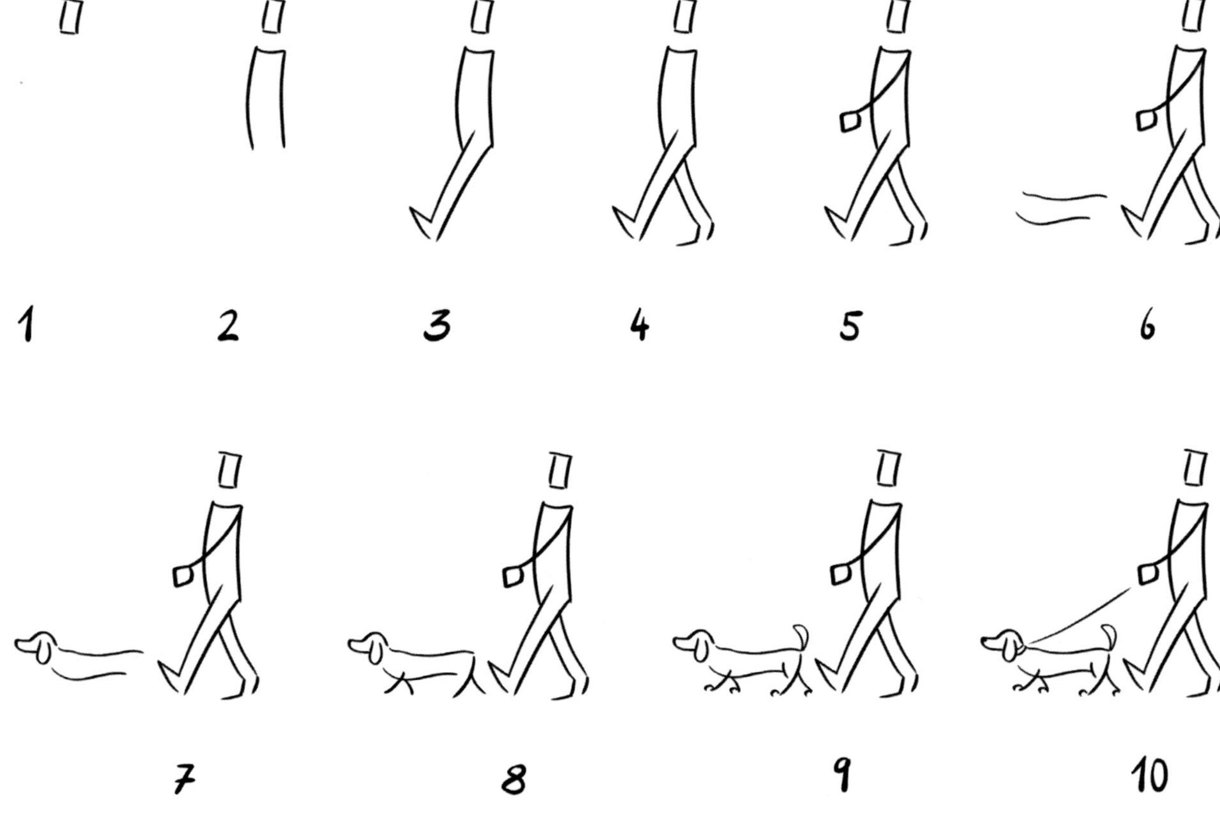

1
2
3
4
5
6
7
8
9
10

DAY 85

Ballet lift

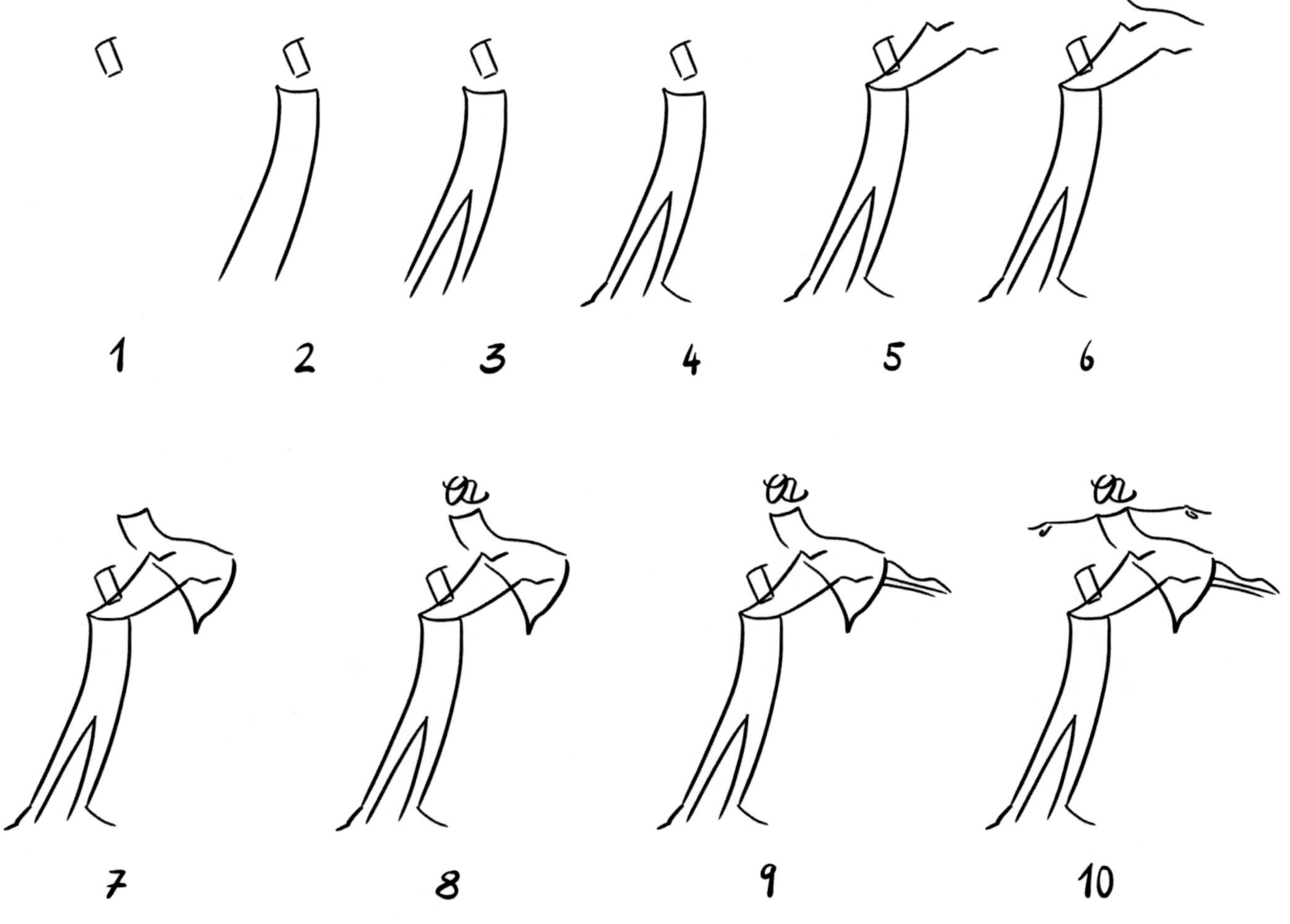

1
2
3
4
5
6
7
8
9
10

DAY 86

Wrestling

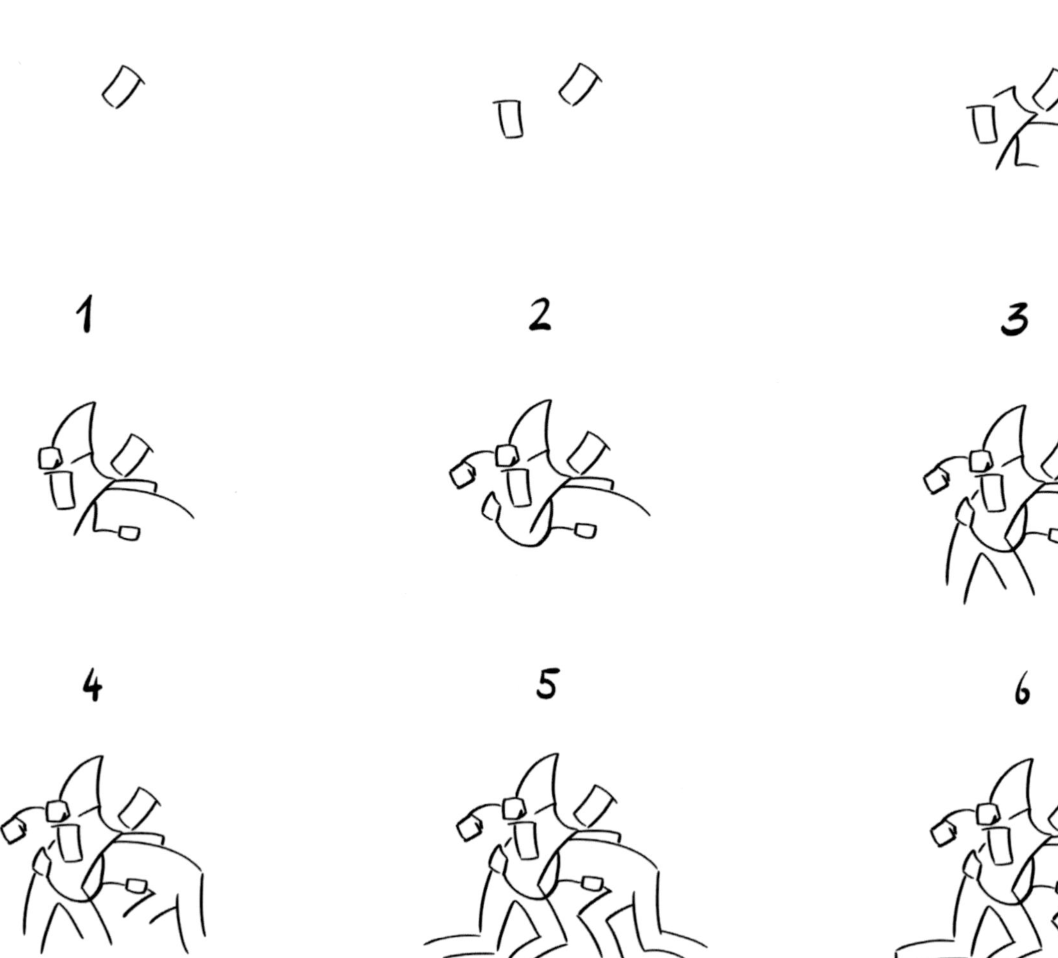
1
2
3
4
5
6
7
8
9

DAY 87

Hugging

1 2 3 4 5

6 7 8 9 10

DAY 88

Playing the violin

1
2
3
4
5
6
7
8
9
10

DAY 89

Chopping wood

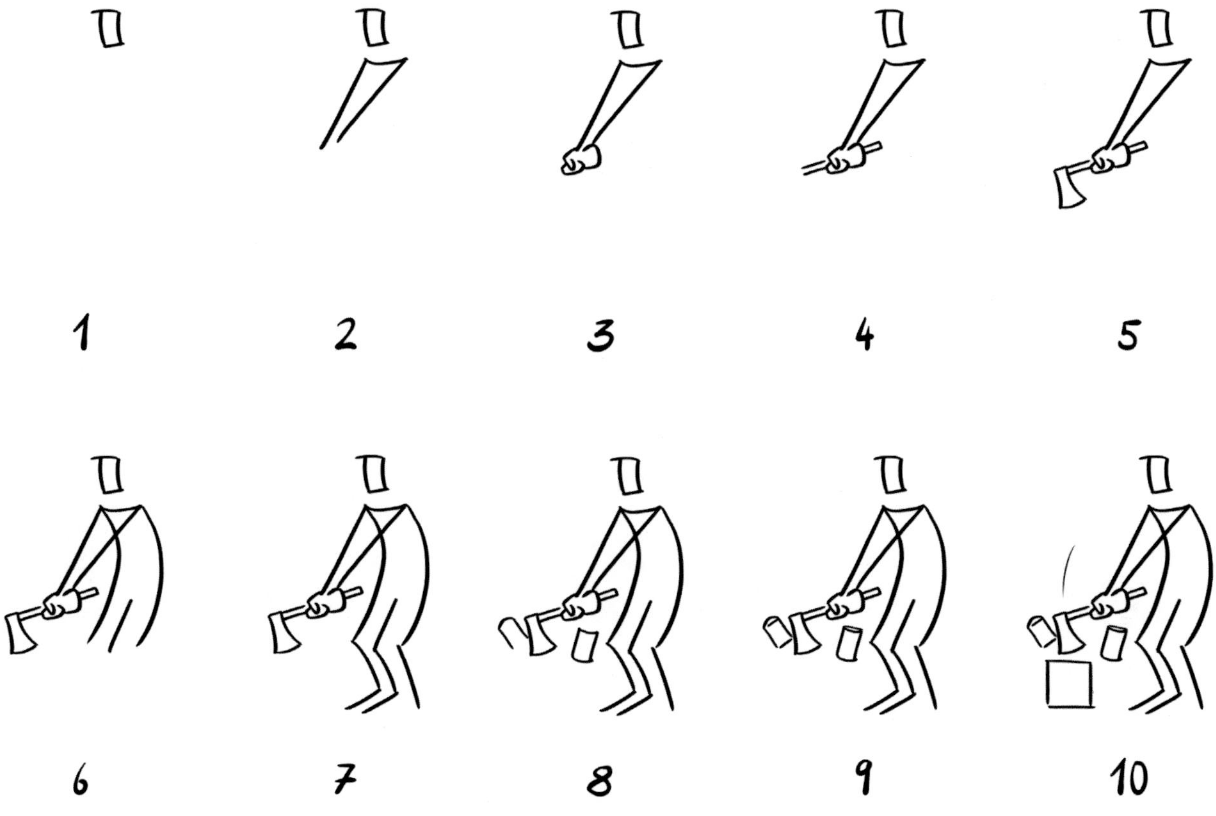

1
2
3
4
5
6
7
8
9
10

DAY 90

Judo

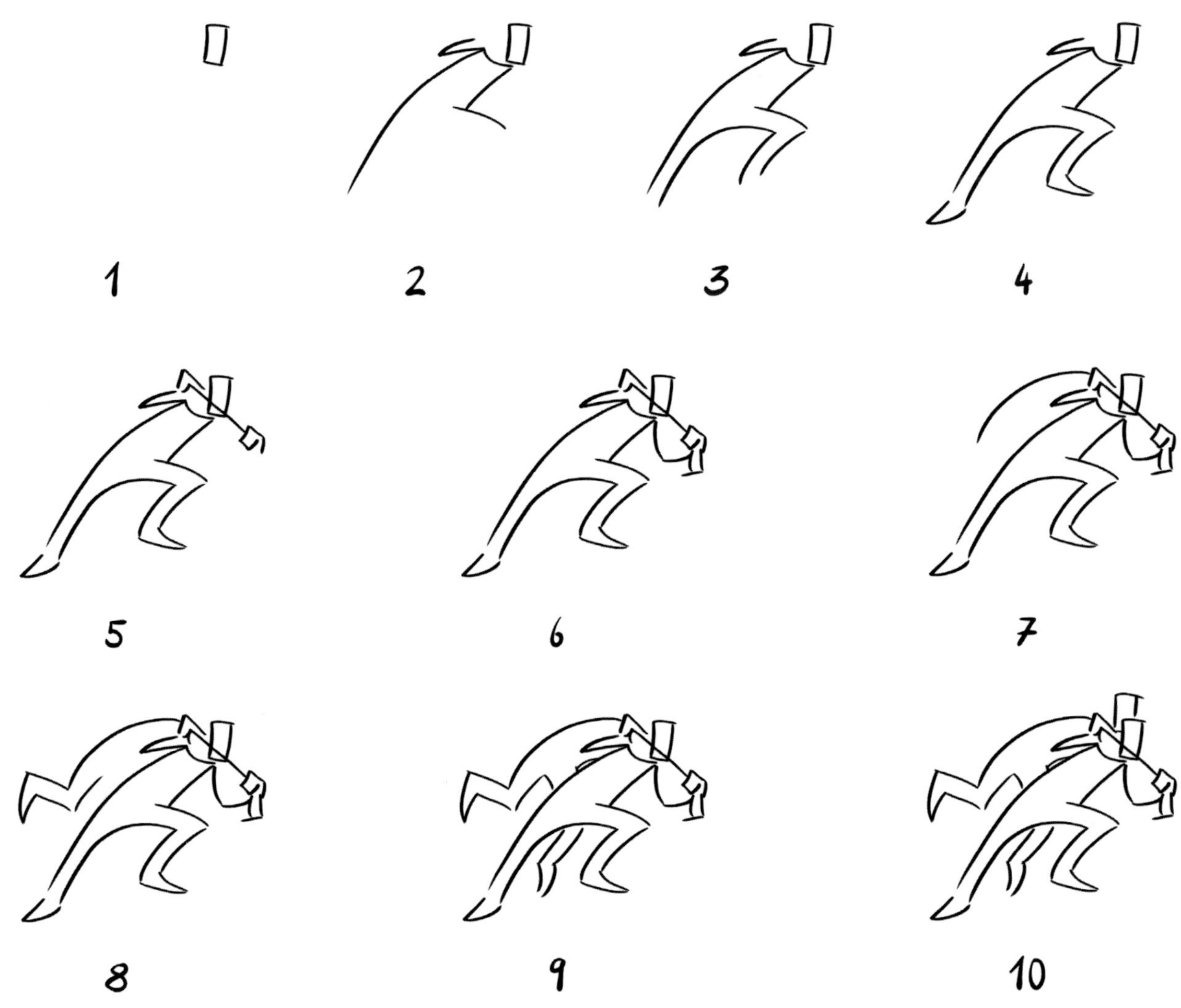

1
2
3
4
5
6
7
8
9
10

DAY 91

Sketching

1 2 3 4

5 6 7 8

9 10 11 12

DAY 92

Sumo wrestler

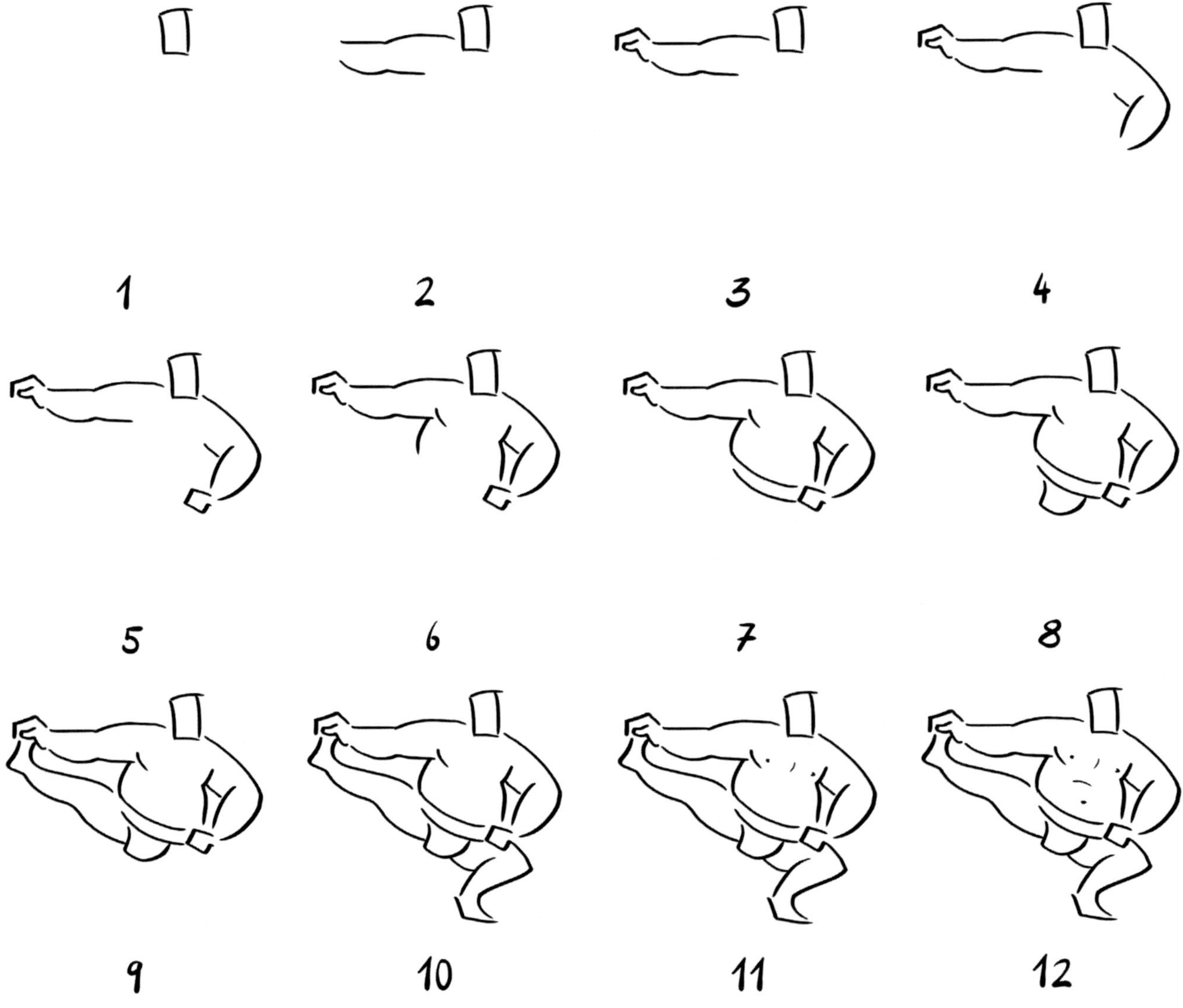

1
2
3
4
5
6
7
8
9
10
11
12

DAY 93

Another sumo wrestler

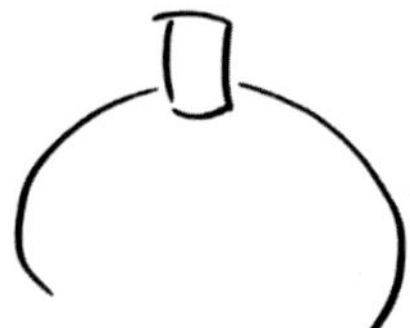

1 2 3 4

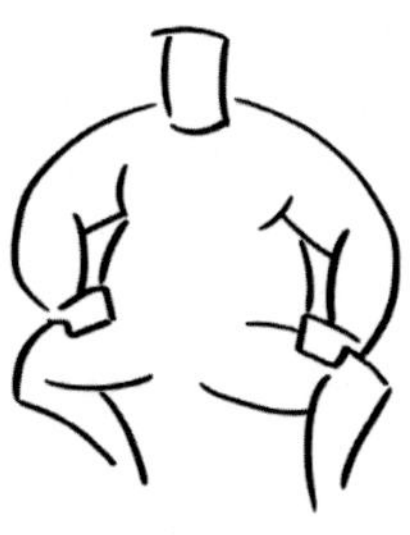

5 6 7 8

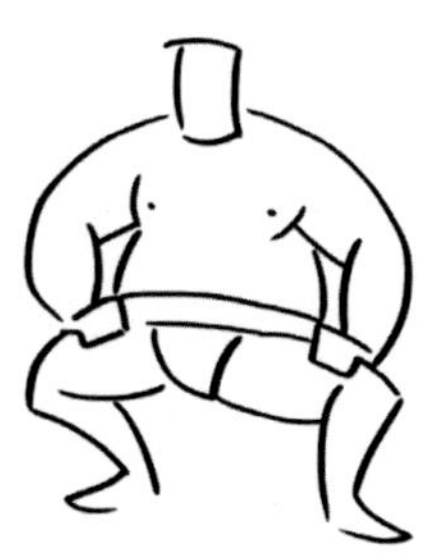

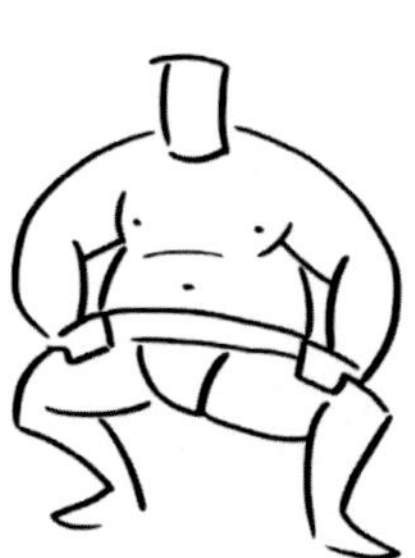

9 10 11 12

DAY 94

Fencing

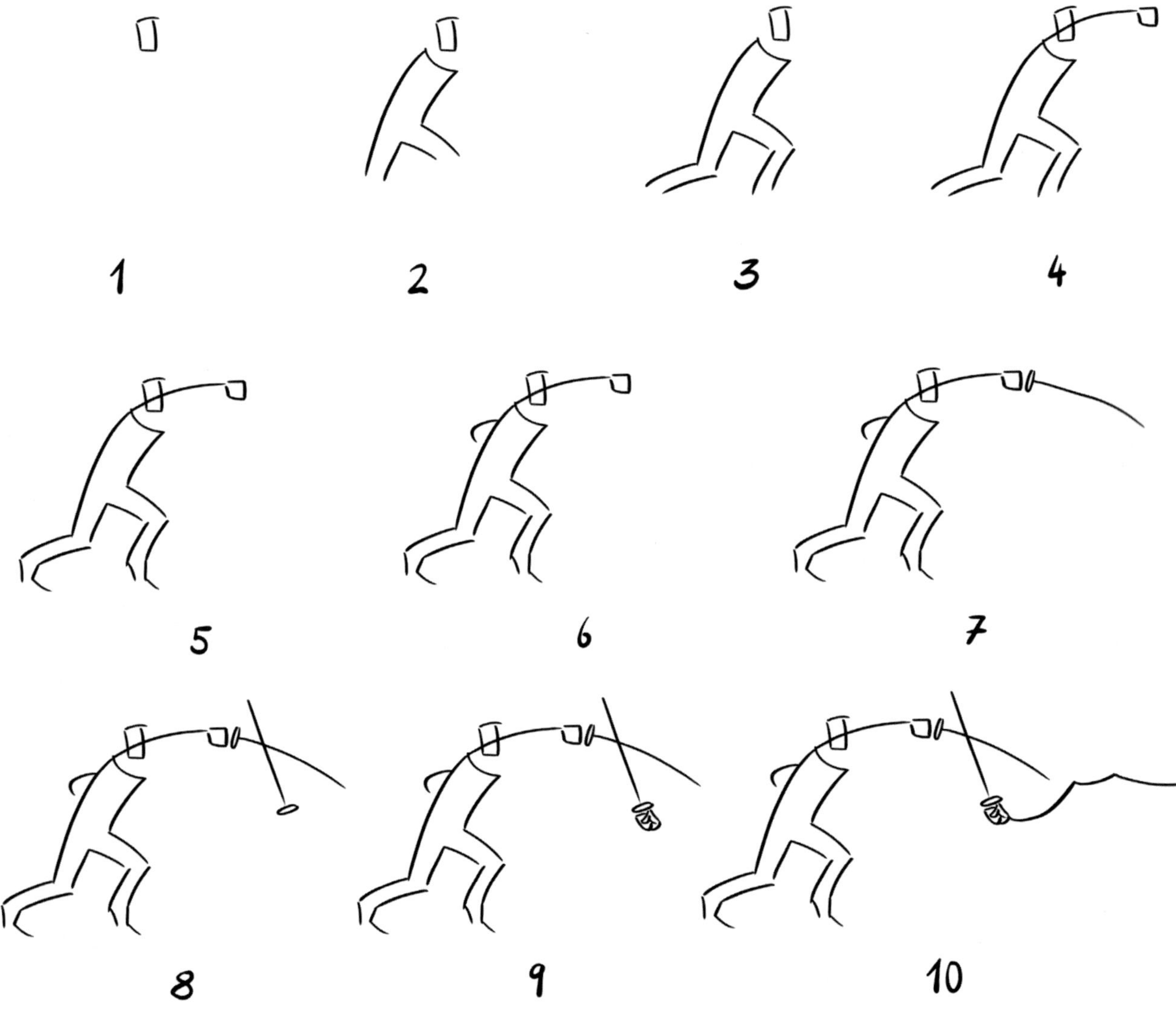

1
2
3
4
5
6
7
8
9
10

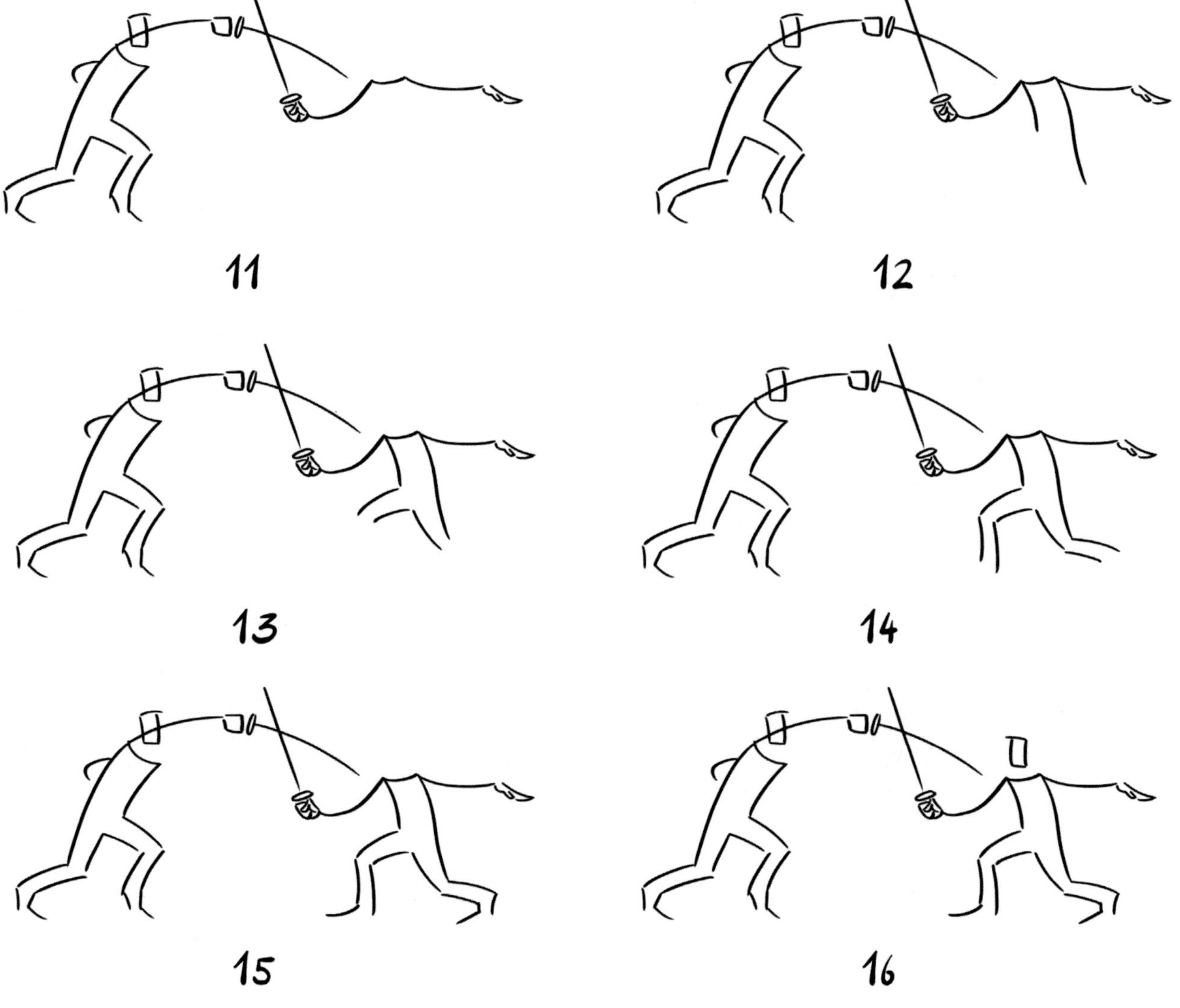
11
12
13
14
15
16

DAY 95

Waltzing

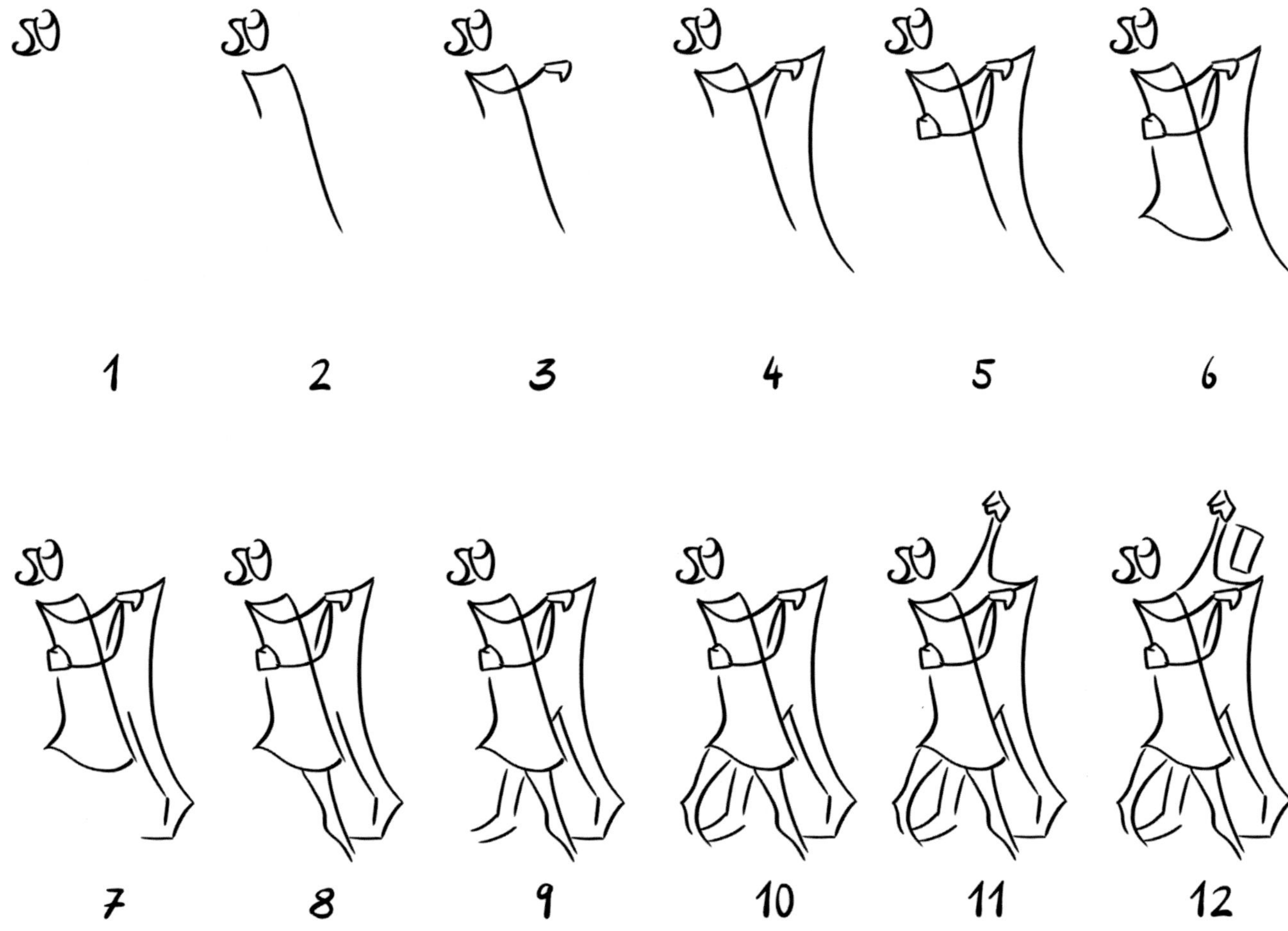

1
2
3
4
5
6
7
8
9
10
11
12

DAY 96

Forging

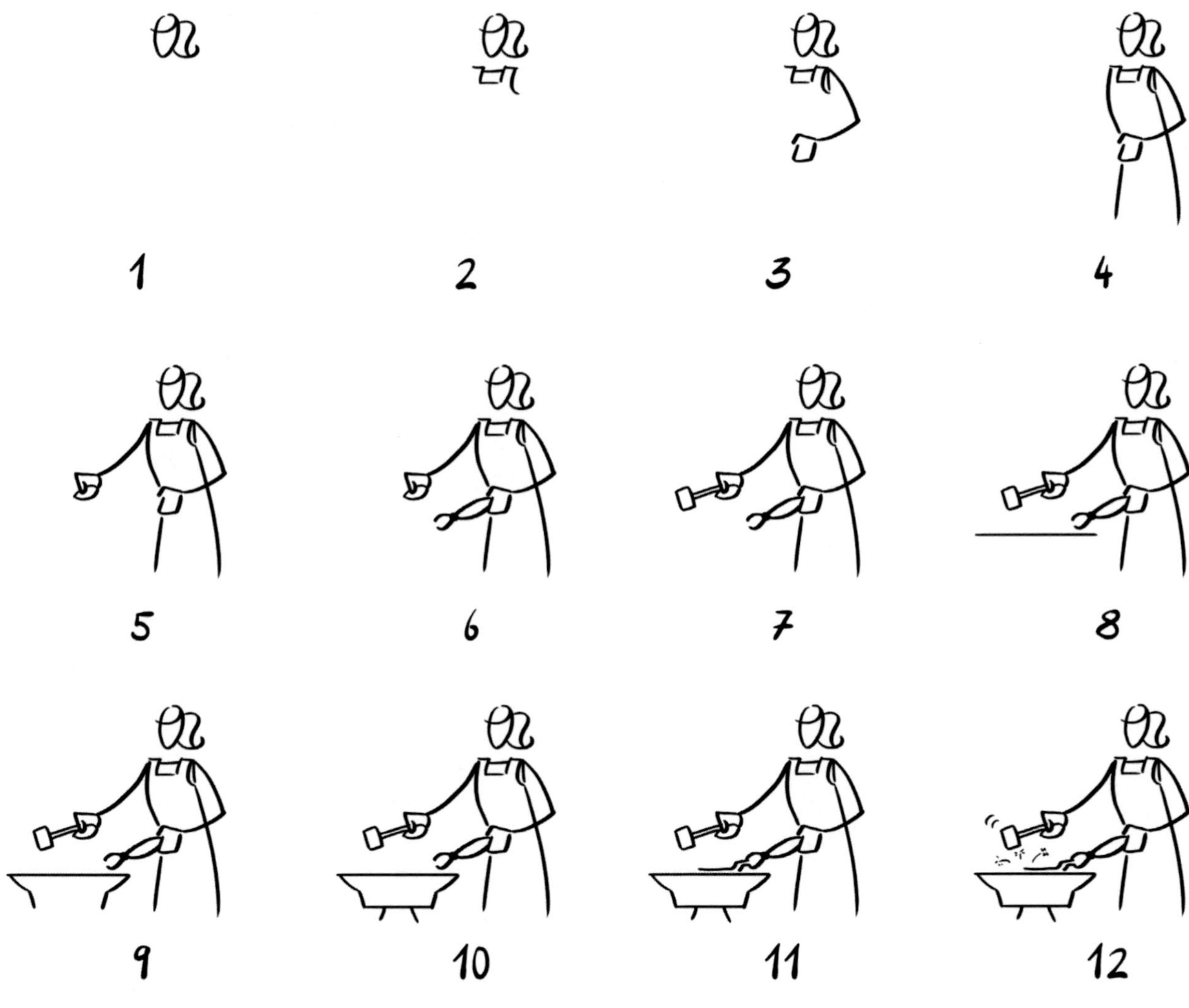
1
2
3
4
5
6
7
8
9
10
11
12

DAY 97

Playing rugby

1 2 3 4

5 6 7 8

9 10 11 12

DAY 98

Playing guitar

1 2 3 4 5

6 7 8 9 10

11 12 13 14

DAY 99

Dancing the tango

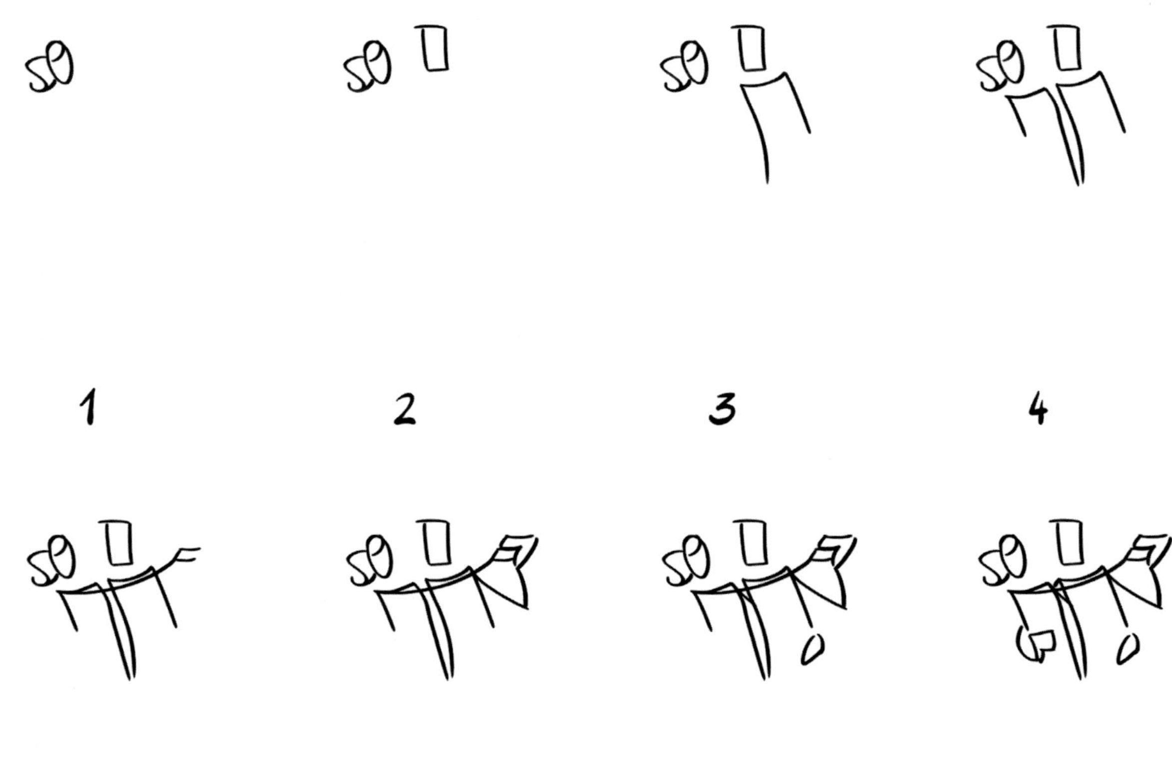
1
2
3
4
5
6
7
8

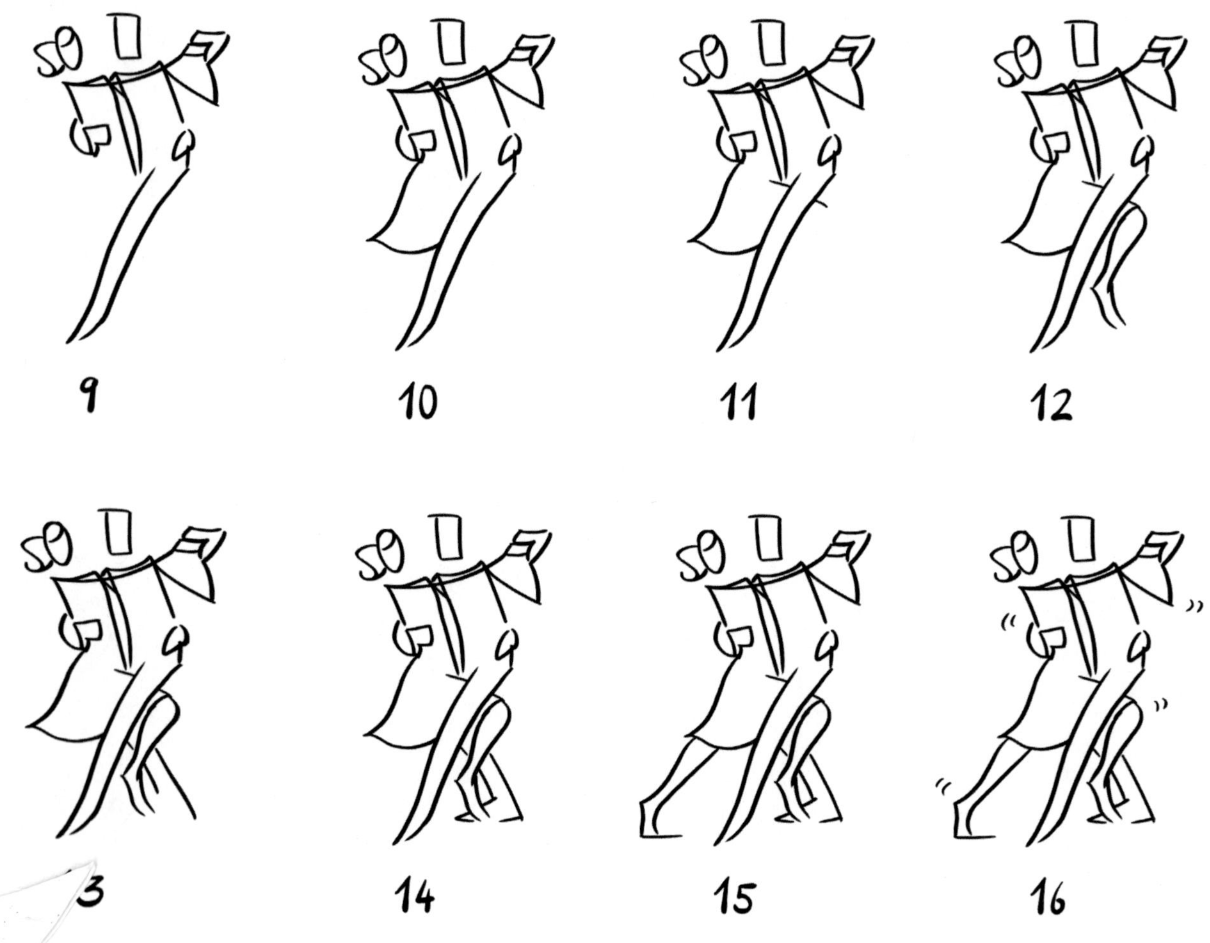
9
10
11
12
3
14
15
16

DAY 100

Kissing

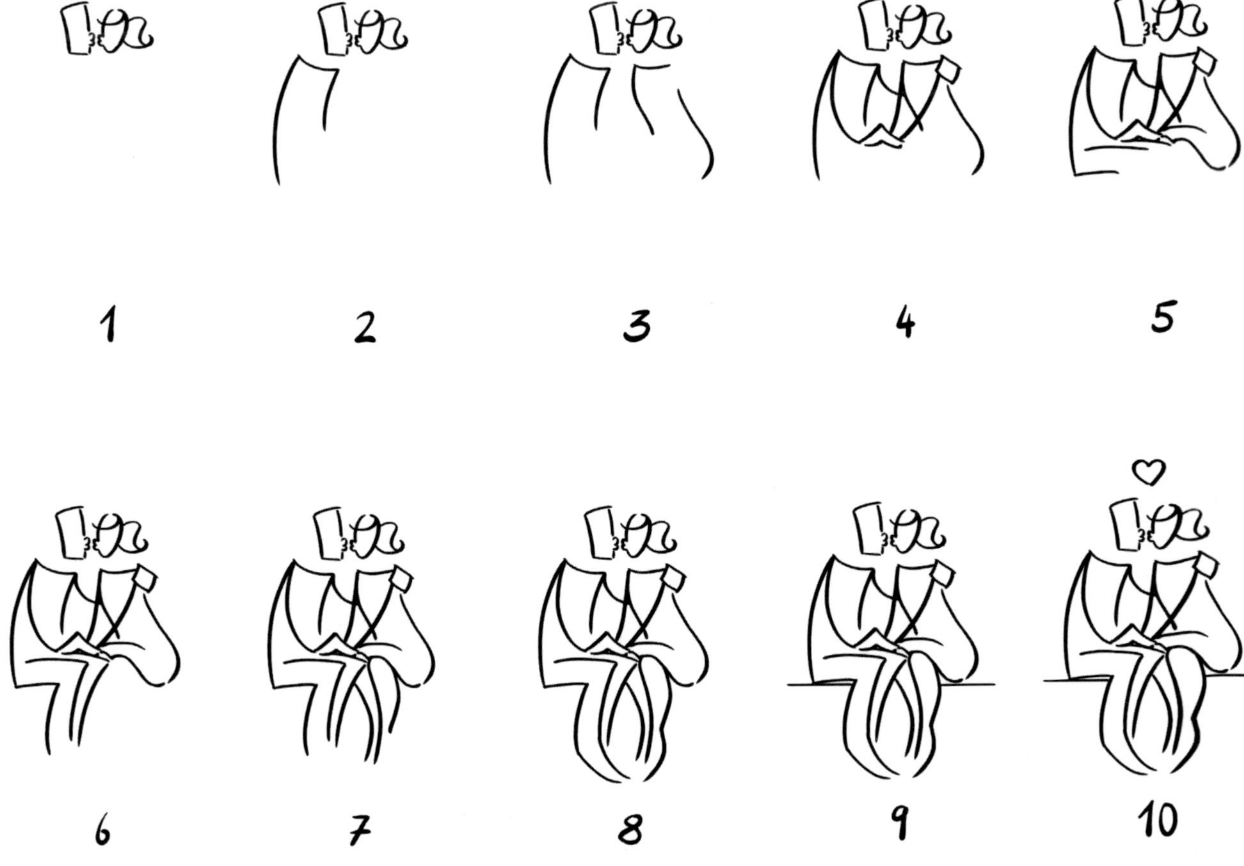
1
2
3
4
5
6
7
8
9
10

THANK YOU

You‘ve done it! You made it the whole way through. Wow! Congratulations. I hope you had fun drawing and learning. As a little parting bonus, you‘ll find a few more general tips for drawings on the last two pages.

I would love to stay in contact with you beyond this book!
So I invite you to sign up to my email list at **holgernilspohl.com/email**
I treat my email list as a conversation and strive to present you with a multitude of tools, thoughts, insights, and reflection questions. And I don‘t mean only business here.
I write about what‘s happening in my life and all of my creative endevours – about visual tools for business and life, and also about my fiction writing in fantasy and kids books.

Lastly, you might want to get the other drawing books I‘ve published in this series if you don‘t have them already: *100 Daily Drawings* and *100 Daily Drawings Vol.2*
You can get them in the form of an ebook from me directly or via Amazon and Kobo. The print versions are available too!
Head over to **holgernilspohl.com/drawingbooks** to get them.

Some tips
for your drawing process

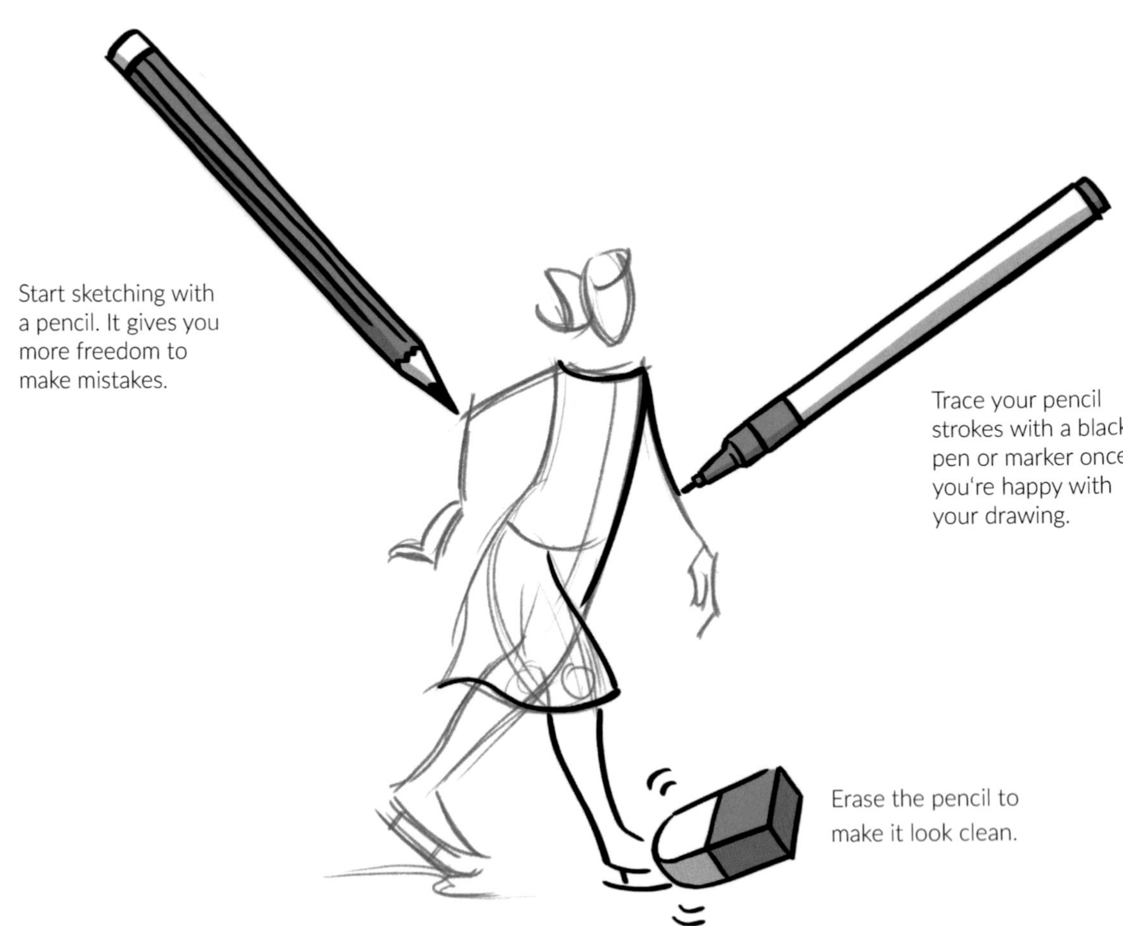

Start sketching with a pencil. It gives you more freedom to make mistakes.
Trace your pencil strokes with a black pen or marker once you're happy with your drawing.
Erase the pencil to make it look clean.

The head is roughly 1/8 the size of the whole body.

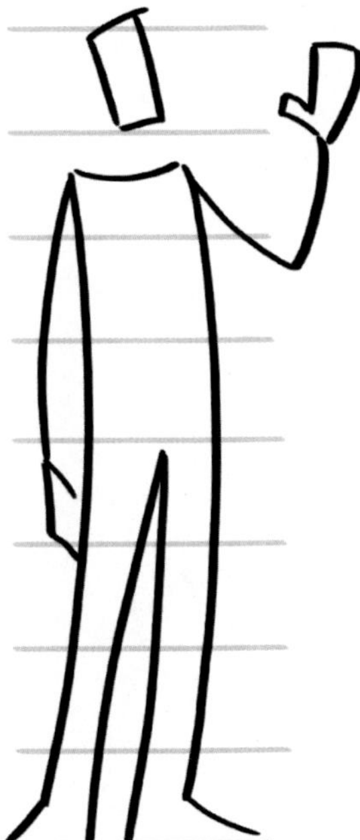

All lines are slightly curved. That's what's making us human compared to a robot. ;)

Hand gestures can give you the variety you need.

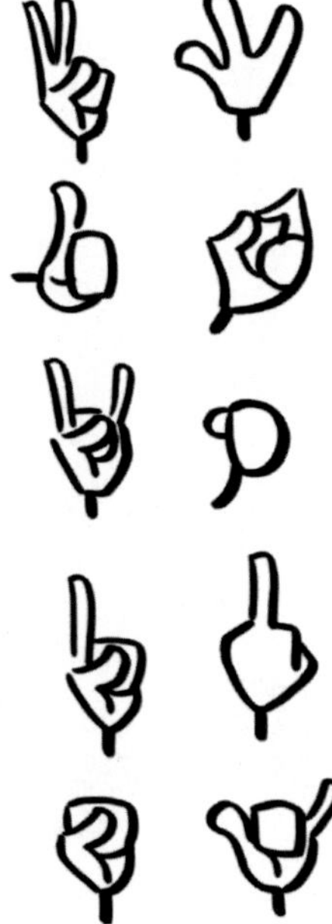

Four positions of the arms can tell most of the things you want to express.

Made in the USA
Middletown, DE
09 October 2022

12342288R00062